Quiet Pictures

Quiet Pictures

Women and Silence in Contemporary British and French Cinema

Sarah Artt

BLOOMSBURY ACADEMIC
NEW YORK • LONDON • OXFORD • NEW DELHI • SYDNEY

BLOOMSBURY ACADEMIC
Bloomsbury Publishing Inc, 1359 Broadway, New York, NY 10018, USA
Bloomsbury Publishing Plc, 50 Bedford Square, London, WC1B 3DP, UK
Bloomsbury Publishing Ireland, 29 Earlsfort Terrace, Dublin 2, D02 AY28, Ireland

BLOOMSBURY, BLOOMSBURY ACADEMIC and the Diana logo are
trademarks of Bloomsbury Publishing Plc

First published in the United States of America 2024
Paperback edition published 2026

Copyright © Sarah Artt, 2024

For legal purposes the Acknowledgments on p. x constitute
an extension of this copyright page.

Cover design by Eleanor Rose
Cover image: *Morvern Callar*, 2002, starring Samantha Morton,
dir. Lynne Ramsay © Entertainment Pictures / Alamy

All rights reserved. No part of this publication may be: i) reproduced or transmitted in any form, electronic or mechanical, including photocopying, recording or by means of any information storage or retrieval system without prior permission in writing from the publishers; or ii) used or reproduced in any way for the training, development or operation of artificial intelligence (AI) technologies, including generative AI technologies. The rights holders expressly reserve this publication from the text and data mining exception as per Article 4(3) of the Digital Single Market Directive (EU) 2019/790.

Bloomsbury Publishing Inc does not have any control over, or responsibility for, any third-party websites referred to or in this book. All internet addresses given in this book were correct at the time of going to press. The author and publisher regret any inconvenience caused if addresses have changed or sites have ceased to exist, but can accept no responsibility for any such changes.

Library of Congress Cataloging-in-Publication Data
Names: Artt, Sarah, author.
Title: Quiet pictures : women and silence in contemporary
British and French cinema / Sarah Artt.
Description: New York : Bloomsbury Academic, 2024. | Includes bibliographical references.
Identifiers: LCCN 2023043249 (print) | LCCN 2023043250 (ebook) |
ISBN 9781501347214 (hardback) | ISBN 9798765113851 (paperback) |
ISBN 9781501347221 (ebook) | ISBN 9781501347238 (pdf)
Subjects: LCSH: Silence in motion pictures. | Women in motion pictures. |
Women motion picture producers and directors. | Motion pictures–France–History. |
Motion pictures–Great Britain–History.
Classification: LCC PN1995.9.S545 A78 2024 (print) |
LCC PN1995.9.S545 (ebook) | DDC 791.43/6115–dc23/eng/20231219
LC record available at https://lccn.loc.gov/2023043249
LC ebook record available at https://lccn.loc.gov/2023043250

ISBN:	HB:	978-1-5013-4721-4
	PB:	979-8-7651-1385-1
	ePDF:	978-1-5013-4723-8
	eBook:	978-1-5013-4722-1

Typeset by Integra Software Services Pvt. Ltd.

For product safety related questions contact productsafety@bloomsbury.com.

To find out more about our authors and books visit www.bloomsbury.com
and sign up for our newsletters.

For George

Contents

List of Figures	viii
Acknowledgments	x
Introduction: More than Absence: Silences in the Cinemas of Joanna Hogg, Lynne Ramsay, Céline Sciamma, and Lucile Hadžhalilović	1
1 Childhood, Curiosity, and Compliance in *Innocence*, *Evolution*, and *Tomboy*	41
2 Adolescence and Collaborative Queer Gazes in *Water Lilies/Naissance des pieuvres,* and *Girlhood/Bande des Filles*	67
3 Artist-Exhibitionists and Silence as Utopian Space in Lynne Ramsay's *Morvern Callar* and Joanna Hogg's *Exhibition*	93
4 Sinister Silences and Mothering in Lynne Ramsay's *We Need to Talk About Kevin* and Lucile Hadžhalilović's *Evolution*	115
5 Silenced Desire and Anger in Joanna Hogg's *Unrelated*, *Archipelago*, and *Exhibition*	137
Afterword	161
References	163
Index	169

Figures

1. Alia's (Hend Sabry) silent scream at the gates of the palace in *Samt al-qusur/The Silences of the Palace* (Moufida Tlatli, 1994) — 18
2. Héloïse (Adèle Haenel) gazes at Marianne — 25
3. Héloïse and Marianne gaze at one another, unsettled by desire — 26
4. Julie (Honor Swinton-Byrne) and Jim (Charlie Heaton) make out in *The Souvenir Part II* — 33
5. Iris (Zoé Auclair, center) is taught to swim by her housemates in *Innocence* — 44
6. Bianca (Bérangère Haubruge) in the fountain at the end of *Innocence* — 50
7. A pupil is shown to the headmistress in *Innocence* — 52
8. Women supervise boys bathing in *Evolution* — 54
9. Nicolas injected in *Evolution* — 56
10. Laure/Mickäel (Zoé Héran) checks their swimsuit silhouette in *Tomboy* — 61
11. Lisa (Jeanne Disson) is goaded by her friends to look inside Laure/Mickäel's shorts in *Tomboy* — 63
12. Marie's underwater view of the synchronized swimmers rehearsing in *Water Lilies* — 72
13. Floriane (Adèle Haenel) sneers at her team mate admonishing her for eating a banana in *Water Lilies* — 75
14. Floriane in discomfort as Marie (Pauline Acquart) inserts her fingers to help rid her of her hymen in *Water Lilies* — 79
15. Another swim team is inspected for "tenue correcte" in *Water Lilies* — 81
16. Lady (Assa Sylla) offers advice to Marieme/Vic (Karidja Touré) in *Girlhood* — 86
17. The "Vic" necklace in *Girlhood* — 87
18. Monica (Dielika Coulibaly) tells Vic they are still a "pute" in *Girlhood* — 88

19	Vic exits the frame at the end of *Girlhood*	91
20	Morvern (Samantha Morton) raises her skirt while standing on the river bank in *Morvern Callar*	102
21	D (Viv Albertine) rifling the horizontal blinds on her office window, as seen from the street	109
22	Eva (Tilda Swinton) ecstatic at La Tomatina in *We Need to Talk About Kevin*	117
23	Kevin's (Ezra Miller) malicious sneer when Eva catches him masturbating in *We Need to Talk About Kevin*	121
24	Eva stares coldly ahead while Franklin (John C. Reilly) cradles infant Kevin in *We Need to Talk About Kevin*	123
25	Eva's ambivalence in the pregnancy yoga changing room in *We Need to Talk About Kevin*	124
26	Kevin and Eva's visual similarities emphasized in *We Need to Talk About Kevin*	126
27	Stella (Roxane Duran) helps Nicolas to breathe underwater in *Evolution*	130
28	Archie (Harry Kershaw), Oakley (Tom Hiddleston), and Jack (Henry Lloyd Hughes) stare at Anna in the pool in *Unrelated*	146
29	Anna (Kathryn Worth) purchasing black lace lingerie in *Unrelated*	148
30	D (Viv Albertine) in beige lace lingerie workshopping a performance in her home studio in *Exhibition*	149
31	Julie (Honor Swinton Byrne) in the black garter belt in *The Souvenir Part I*	149
32	Oakley observes Anna at dinner in *Unrelated*	151
33	Patricia (Kate Fahy) and Christopher (Christopher W. Baker) in conversation in *Archipelago*	157

Acknowledgments

This book has been a long time in the making. I am grateful to so many people for their kindness, support, and friendship during the writing of this work. I wish to thank Edinburgh Napier University for giving me a sabbatical in 2016 which allowed me to prepare the proposal, and for sending me on two separate writing retreats which were crucial to the development and completion of this book.

My treasured colleagues (past and present) in the English team at Edinburgh Napier—you all rock.

Emily Alder, Elsa Bouet, Arin Keeble, David Pellegrini, and Tara Thomson generously read sections of this book at key junctures. I'm very grateful to each of you for your encouragement and feedback.

To my parents, Tom and Suzanne, and to my in-laws, Colin and Muriel Williamson—I'm so grateful for your love and support throughout my life.

To the people who didn't realize they were influential to my thinking about parts of this book: thank you for the gifts of your beauty, your desires, and most of all your (not always silent) gazes.

To Elsa, Emily, and Tara: without your friendship, love, and intellectual companionship I would never have finished this book.

Introduction
More than Absence: Silences in the Cinemas of Joanna Hogg, Lynne Ramsay, Céline Sciamma, and Lucile Hadžhalilović

In *Nightwood*, Djuna Barnes gives silence a quality: "her silence, as if speech were heavy and unclarified" (1936: 107). Being silent and being looked at: the twin experiences of what it means to be a woman on screen. Modernist and experimental writers like Barnes and Jean Rhys have been the experts at articulating these experiences of silence that are anything but uniform. In their literary work, the textures of women's silence come to the fore and we can access their characters' thoughts about the choice to be silent, or when they are deliberately silenced by the circumstances in which they find themselves. These textures of silence can take several forms: silent observation, and being talked over or admonished into silence are frequent occurrences, but there are also instances where bodily gestures can stand in for words. In Rhys's devastating first novel *Quartet*, the protagonist Marya is shocked into silence by her friend Lois's aggressive husband who declares his sexual obsession with her: "She stared at him, silent … she felt despair and a sort of hard rage. 'It's all wrong,' she thought. 'Everything's wrong'" (Rhys 57). Though she does not remain silent, this articulation of what Marya feels but does not say constitutes a significant moment. Here, we are given access to the inner texture and quality of one woman's silence.

Marina Warner, writing about Carrington's life and work, makes the following observation: "to experience woman's doubled identity, feeling the eyes of others on her, identifying with them as they comment on her looks and her demeanour, and, as often as not, disapprove of her" (2017: 150). This evokes an experience common to many women: the anxiety of knowing you is being watched and sometimes judged. In many ways, the articulation of these experiences that we find in the work of these writers aligns with critiques of Laura Mulvey's initial theorization of to-be-looked-at-ness: the woman on screen as glamorous object, "the silent image of woman still tied to her place as bearer, not maker of meaning" (Mulvey 59).

But what does it mean if that Mulveyan person returns that look? What does it mean if the gaze can be something mutual, even collaborative? And what does the quality of women's silence mean when it is represented to us both visually and aurally? Contemporaries of Mulvey, such as Annette Kuhn and Teresa de Lauretis, both questioned this position of the woman who is unable to return the look, permanently silenced by the place assigned to her in the symbolic order of classical Hollywood cinema. My provocation in this book is that there are films that have succeeded in portraying various textures of silence, offering a variety of looks, stares, and ultimately offering up a different kind of gaze via a more varied portrayal of silence by allowing these silent gazes to occupy significant space on screen. I want to argue that silence is a feminist aesthetic, part of "the process of making the invisible visible" (Citron et al. 1978: 103). As Marta Zarzycka notes in her study of the "sound" of war photography, "women in many cultures have used the aural as a means of both re-appropriation and empowerment" (2013: 44). This is precisely what Lucile Hadžhalilović, Joanna Hogg, Lynne Ramsay, and Céline Sciamma do in their film work.

These are directors who make deliberate use of silence in order to portray what it means to exist as a woman. While silence has long been a component of women's cinema, silence as a deliberate aesthetic strategy has not been fully examined in spite of Susan Sontag's assertion that silence remains a form of communication vital to contemporary art. In *Unrelated* (Hogg, 2007), *Archipelago* (Hogg, 2010), *Exhibition* (Hogg, 2013), *The Souvenir Part I* and *II* (Hogg, 2019 and 2021), *Morvern Callar* (Ramsay, 2002), *We Need to Talk About Kevin* (Ramsay, 2011), *Innocence* (Hadžhalilović, 2004), *Evolution* (Hadžhalilović, 2015), *Water Lilies/Naissance des Pieuvres* (Sciamma, 2007), *Tomboy* (Sciamma, 2011), *Girlhood/Bande des Filles* (Sciamma, 2014), *Portrait of a Lady on Fire/Portrait d'une jeune fille en feu* (Sciamma, 2019), and *Petite Maman/Little Mother* (Sciamma, 2021), silence is not always represented as a character remaining mute or expressionless; the silence of these films is one of introspection, and contemplation; it can indicate the unseen, but it can also be a tool for examining unspoken or still taboo topics, such as anger, loss, and desire, as well as feelings of ambivalence (particularly in relation to motherhood). Silence and quiet also make space for the representation of collaborative gazes that represent shared desires that may not always be articulated verbally.

Too often, a trip to the cinema can be advocated as a way to force oneself to "switch off," as the cinema remains a space where silence is desired alongside opportunities for less distracted viewing. And yet, when it comes to certain kinds of filmmaking, we must account for the possibility of being confronted with textures and atmospheres of silence that are anything but restful. Stuart Sim argues, "There are few things more calculated to prompt the interpretive faculty into action than the presence of silence in an artistic context" (111–12). The films of Hogg, Sciamma, Hadžhalilović, and Ramsay use silence to create focus in a variety of ways. The focus may be on a single character, aspect, or image. Silence can work in the way Sim and Sontag suggest, to focus the mind and gaze of the spectator. Silence can also work as a space to show shared, desiring gazes that are present in a number of the films here.

Silence in a Noisy Age

Silence is sometimes considered harmful and complicit. Act-Up's slogan of the AIDS pandemic Silence=Death, or the equally memorable phrase from Audre Lorde "Your silence will not protect you" (2017: 2) both strike this chord, that to remain silent is to fail to act in solidarity. Both Act-Up's and Lorde's ideas remind us of what it means to remain silent under patriarchy. More recently, Rebecca Solnit has also written about the equation of silence and complicity. But silence is something that has many facets and qualities. Consider Lorde's assertion—this clearly applies to scenarios where speaking out about injustice is essential. Yet, her phrase can also be interpreted in other ways, as a rallying cry for living an authentic life that acknowledges the truth of one's own feelings and impulses. Ignoring or silencing one's more troubling feelings does not make those feelings not exist. Silencing does not protect us from the occurrence of those feelings, and what matters is how we acknowledge and deal with them in our everyday lives, and in turn how we see them expressed through art and culture.

What interests me in relation to the work of these directors is how silence becomes more than its current cultural parameters and why it is important to trace the various ways in which silence can be used, and to examine its relationship to power. There is a substantial legacy of silence as a technique used predominantly by women filmmakers from a range of global locations, yet no book has yet made a study of this. I have chosen to focus my attention on the work of these four directors because their outputs are modest but powerful, and when I began this work, neither Sciamma nor Hogg had achieved the kind of high-profile visibility that has come with the critical successes of *Portrait of a Lady on Fire* or *The Souvenir Part I* and *II*. I also wanted to bring Sciamma's and Hogg's work into dialogue with the far less known work of Hadžhalilović, whose films continue to prove unsettling and uncanny, walking the border with horror without running headlong into that genre. My interest in silence as a texture very much began with Ramsay's *Morvern Callar*, and despite the fact that her work has been critically lauded, she has never been as prolific in her feature film work as one might expect. My hope is that *Quiet Pictures* will initiate further work on up-and-coming filmmakers from a greater range of global locations who are deploying textures of silence. In "The Aesthetics of Silence" Sontag asserts that silence is a choice the artist makes that is, in turn, discernible to the audience. I want to unpack the consequences of Sontag's ideas here, and apply them directly to cinema. Sontag also notes that silence comes equipped with certain assumptions: "the most common, and dubious version of the notion of silence ... invokes the idea of 'the ineffable'" (Sontag 30). This association poses particular problems for women, since it aligns with representations of woman as a symbol, as an object of contemplation, and suggests an unproblematized acceptance of Mulvey's initial assessment of the restricted ways of being seen typically offered to women in mainstream cinema. It is therefore a temptation to simply see silence in films made by women as part of this long and difficult cultural legacy of the mysterious, unknowable terrain of femininity. This book seeks to examine the ways in which these four contemporary women filmmakers are making silence into something more than an erasure.

Silence can also be uncomfortable, and this is one of the reasons we often seek to obliterate it in everyday life. But this discomfort is also part of silence's disruptive power. Even when it is deployed in the service of activism, silence is often a space that people rush to fill, or it must be constrained in its duration as it is when used in ceremonies of commemoration and mourning. Silence in the cinema is used to express a multitude of emotions and situations and by looking at silence in relation to the representation of women on screen at different stages in their lives, we can begin to understand some of these various uses of silence. This study will therefore examine characters as children, adolescents, and in early and late adulthood, alongside the various ways silence is used, whether as the absence of dialogue, or the deliberate muting of the soundtrack. While absence and muting are two of the most legible technical interventions, I will also be considering silence in relation to feelings and desires that remain unspoken.

Slowness and Silence

Related to this question of silence as technique is the deployment of slowness. Lutz Koepnick argues that "slowness asks viewers to take time and explore what our contemporary culture of speed rarely allows us to ask, namely what it means to live in a present that no longer knows one integrated dynamic, grand narrative, or stable point of observation" (4). Salomé Voegelin makes a related claim for silence—that it is "the space at the basis of all sound" (Voegelin 98) and that it is "the beginning of listening" (83). For these directors, slowness combined with silence is often the beginning of looking and listening for both characters and audiences. Silence provides the opportunity to begin to look, to develop a gaze that sees the world and oneself in it. It is also an opportunity to listen and to feel. These uses of silence permit moving beyond to-be-looked-at-ness, and even moving beyond the idea of simply returning the male gaze, since many of these collaborative gazes take place between women, or between femme and non-binary people. Silence and slowness create space: for looking, for listening, for bodies to take on new ways of being seen.

> Silence is the artist's ultimate other-worldly gesture; by silence he [sic] frees himself from servile bondage to the world, which appears as patron, client, consumer, antagonist, arbiter, and distorter of his work.
>
> (Sontag 6)

Here, Sontag is writing about artists and philosophers who fall silent, in the sense that after a certain point they no longer make new work. Their critical and artistic voice falls silent, while previous work continues to "speak" to new audiences. We might also consider this in light of musicians (living or dead) whose back catalogue continues to inspire, to be re mixed, covered, or otherwise distributed. While we no longer have new work from Prince, his music continues to offer us joy and connection, and in this sense his legacy will never be entirely silent. Sontag's idea of silence as the other-worldly gesture also configures silence as a final gesture, signifying disgust or simply exhaustion. Yet, Sontag notes that this kind of gesture of falling silent also tends to lend the existing body of work "a certificate of unchallengeable seriousness" (6). This certainly typifies the role of silence in art cinema, where an absence of dialogue is so often treated as the ultimate artistic gesture of seriousness. Anyone who has ever read or written for a film festival program will be familiar with the too easy deployment of phrases like "hauntingly beautiful," which often operate as a code for films that might be boring, or soporific, or otherwise painfully earnest in their deployment of silence.

What I wish to explore here is how silence is being taken up in a variety of different ways by these four directors. Certainly, their work is serious in the sense that the stories are dramatic and sincere rather than comic in tone. But silence takes on a number of qualities beyond the convention of the great artist who has decided they have nothing more to say to the world. What I want to take from Sontag's thoughts here is the idea of *gestures of silence which belong to the protagonists of these films*. In *Morvern Callar*, Lynne Ramsay shows us what it means to inhabit a freely chosen silence. Morvern (Samantha Morton) is allowed to do just what Sontag says the artist can do, she "frees [her]self from servile bondage to the world" and it is this freedom that allows her to pursue silence further, and to become someone who is perceived as an artist. Rather than the end of creativity, silence has always been a rich part of Morvern's world. In the films of Céline Sciamma, silence tends to be the position from which young people take in their surroundings, and this is particularly common for her young women protagonists, as well as those whose gender is fluid or in transition, as with Laure/Mikaël in *Tomboy* and Marieme/Vic in *Bande des Filles*. Silence is the space for looking in Sciamma's work, where we are asked to contemplate the importance of how and what these young protagonists see. Sciamma's young protagonists look and stare but they also share collaborative, intimate gazes with friends and lovers, and as spectators their silence compels us to give them our attention.

> Consider the difference between *looking* and *staring*. A look is voluntary, it is also mobile, rising and falling, in intensity as its foci of interest are taken up and then exhausted. A stare has, essentially, the character of a compulsion, it is steady, unmodulated, "fixed." Traditional art invites a look. Art that is silent engenders a stare. Silent art allows –at least in principle–no release from attention, because there has never been any soliciting of it. A stare is perhaps as far from history, as close to eternity, as contemporary art can get.
>
> (Sontag 16)

It would be interesting to know what Sontag would have made of Marina Abramović's 2010 performance *The Artist Is Present*[1] where patrons of New York's Museum of Modern Art queued for hours for the chance to share a gaze with Abramović. This work, as well as her *512 Hours* performed at London's Serpentine Gallery in 2014, is a performance which depends on an atmosphere of quietude and silence from the artist herself, from her collaborators, and from her audience. Writing in *The New York Times*, Holland Cotter describes the core of Abramović's performance in *The Artist Is Present* as both a stare and a gaze. Cotter, perhaps searching for a term beyond the catch-all category of performance art, describes this silent sitting as "basically a 700-hour silent opera." His comparison with an art form that is anything but silent is telling: it suggests that Abramović's silent sharing of something between a look and

---

[1] Holland Cotter. "700 Hour Silent Opera Reaches Finale at MoMa," May 30, 2010. *The New York Times*. http://www.nytimes.com/2010/05/31/arts/design/31diva.html [accessed January 31, 2017].

a stare is deeply layered, and that it depends on a certain openness on the part of the artist and the participants who sit opposite her. All performance requires collaboration and trust, but opera in particular is a highly theatrical combination of music, singing, costume, and performance. The enormous audience for Abramović's silent sitting and the desire for the chance to share a moment of connection with her are a confirmation that silence has many performative and emotive qualities, and that each encounter with the artist will feel different for each participant, that there is something unique in the silence and the gaze they share. In the documentary *The Artist Is Present* (Matthew Ackers and Jeff Dupre, 2012) a particularly significant encounter is captured, where Abramovic is seemingly surprised by the appearance of Ulay, her former collaborator. When he sits down in front of her in the foyer of MoMA, she is visibly moved to tears, and reaches out to take both his hands, a gesture that she does not make to any other participant. The audience breaks into rapturous applause and cheers at this gesture, which signals the power of that shared gaze, and the significance of their personal and artistic history. The addition of touch as an aspect of the shared gaze marks out this moment as particularly intimate.

Sontag is right: silence is a choice the artist makes, and that silence can be deemed highly valuable by an audience, whether they are watching a performance or participating in other ways. It is not simply about the seriousness of falling silent after a lifetime of words. By offering up spaces of quietude and silence, Abramović's work deals in the importance of connection, not just the chance to be in the artist's presence, but to silently share something that is intangible, ephemeral, but no less meaningful. The shared silence of *512 Hours*, which made patrons put all their belongings (particularly their camera phones) in lockers before entering the silent, white space of the Serpentine Gallery, created a similar atmosphere of purity and contemplation. Purity and contemplation are both highly traditional aspects to silence when it is associated with devotional or religious practices such as silent prayer, silent retreats, and meditation. The quest for silence is something that preoccupies not only artists like Abramović and the filmmakers under discussion here, but a number of writers who have published books about silence over the last decade.

Popular Silence

A spate of texts have emerged in recent years extolling not just the pleasures of seeking out quietude and silence, but arguing for its necessity as an aspect of well-being. These works approach silence in various ways, including it as an aspect of spiritual devotion, philosophy, and an environmental concern, but they are all driven by the authors' intense desire to experience silence.

Writers interested in the history of silence tend to inevitably reference both John Cage's composition 4'33 and anechoic chambers as extreme experiences of silence. John Bigunet is keen to point out that absolute silence is truly unsettling: "The quietest place on earth, an anechoic chamber at Orfield Laboratories in Minnesota, is so quiet that the longest anybody has been able to bear it is 45 minutes" (2015: 19). George Michelsen Foy in *Zero Decibels: The Quest for Absolute Silence* is one of the few people who can not only withstand the anechoic chamber, but, as he notes, "it was soothing to be in there ... I really would have liked to stay longer in Orfield's chamber" (2010: 148). Clearly, there is some difference of opinion on the effect of total silence, and how pleasurable or unpleasurable it can be to experience it.

There are several other books about silence released around the same time as Michelsen Foy's (2010) and Biguenet's (2015): Stuart Sim's *Manifesto for Silence* (2007), Sara Maitland's *A Book of Silence* (2008), and George Prochnik's *In Pursuit of Silence* (2011). These books all offer evidence of popular interest in silence as an aspect of personal well-being, alongside the current noisy world we all inhabit. They demonstrate that silence is a quality worth noticing well beyond the confines of the academy, and they offer a sense of how audiences might perceive and experience silence.

Biguenet's book is a series of ruminations on the meaning of silence, and how it differs from like-sounding concepts such as solitude. Like most of his fellow authors on silence, he is keen to point out that silence has "value in a clamourous world" (6). This implies that noise has now become the baseline for existence, certainly for those of us who inhabit urban areas. Therefore, opportunities for silence have become increasingly coveted. As an example, Biguenet comments on the place of silence in relation to air travel: "Silence, in my experience, takes two forms in the air: luxury and terror" (14). The more one pays for higher classes of air travel, the more one is essentially paying to be insulated from noise: that of machinery, and that of other people. However, prolonged silence in the air can also be eerie; an absence of familiar sounds or reassuring announcements is an indication that something has gone catastrophically wrong. In many ways, this example crystallizes the poles of the significance of silence: it can be soothing, or frightening.

Sara Maitland's *A Book of Silence* deals with the author's desire to seek out silence after a very noisy life filled with family and lively debate. Maitland traces a range of fascinating scenarios in which silence occurs, from the experiences of solo explorers, to that of religious hermits. She also examines her own increasing desire for silence as she ages, particularly during the decade leading up to menopause. This "hunting" for silence that Maitland examines fits well with my own interest in the relationship between these cinematic instances of silence and women at different stages in their lives. Like Bigunet, Maitland discusses the relationship between silence and solitude, which for her are deeply similar: "They both refer to that space in which both the social self and the ego dissolve into a kind of hyper-awareness where sound and particularly language gets in the way" (2008: 17). This idea of language "getting in the way" is particularly salient to the films under discussion here. Silence becomes a rich space of potential, a place of exploration for the protagonists in these films. For the girls of Hadžhalilović's *Innocence* silence is what allows their gaze to develop, and to realize that there is a world beyond the walls of their school grounds. In Ramsay's *Morvern Callar*, we inhabit Morvern's rich inner world as she creates her own sonic landscape which often omits speech. Marieme/Vic in Sciamma's *Bande des Filles* realizes their potential for agency in the silence of the family kitchen when they take their brother's knife and decide to join a gang. For Anna, the protagonist of Joanna Hogg's *Unrelated*, silence functions in a somewhat different way: it contains isolation, hidden pain, and her sensuality.

Maitland comments further on some of the negative associations that have developed around silence: "We have reached a point in contemporary Western culture where we believe that too much silence is either 'mad' (depressive, escapist, weird) or 'bad' (selfish, antisocial) and I found I had internalised quite a lot of this way of thinking" (2008: 25). Just like Maitland, Anna in *Unrelated* also seems to have internalized these ideas about silence; throughout the film she chats frequently in a way that completely deflects any sense of reflection or inner turmoil. Initially, Anna (Kathryn Worth) does not want to be found out or prodded about displaying "too much silence." Verena (Mary Roscoe) notices this almost immediately, reproaching Anna for her reticence: "You haven't told me anything."

When it comes to unsettling silences on screen, Hadžhalilović's work is exemplary. Her first two films, *Innocence* and *Evolution*, contain the silences of very young characters confronted with deeply troubling events. The girls in *Innocence* dance before an unseen audience, and are then brought out of their enclosed world at the end of the film to confront the contemporary moment where they will become aware of their sexual image. In *Evolution*, silence characterizes the strange hospital visits experienced by the young boys and the women who care for them in an isolated island community. Her third film, *Earwig* (2021), is similar in tone, filled with scenes set in a dark, quiet house, following the days of an isolated and largely silent young girl with teeth made of ice, and the man who cares for her. In all three films, children's fears are never articulated verbally but we are left to share in their silent observation of the world.

When Sara Maitland embarks on a solo retreat to the isle of Skye, she finds herself confronting many of the more troubling aspects of silence, particularly when it is accompanied by being alone and in solitude, and what she uncovers is not dissimilar to the silence encountered in Hadžhalilović's work. One of Maitland's most startling remarks about her time on Skye is: "the silence itself unskinned me" (54). This speaks to the aspects of silence that are both revelatory and unsettling for the individual, the idea that silence can help us to confront our true nature, but that this is not always a positive experience. In 2018, I visited some of the locations on Lanzarote where Hadžhalilović shot *Evolution*. The volcanic landscape and near-deserted villages offered nothing in the way of comfort, and I found it was a landscape filled with bizarre angles, and muffling stones. To describe these places as desolate is perhaps unfair, but the lack of other noises from animals or vegetation proved surprisingly strange. In this peculiar experience of silence, I kept returning to an idea from Julia Kristeva's *Powers of Horror*, where she quotes from Céline's *Journey to the End of Night* "on est puceau de l'horreur, comme on est puceau de la volupté [we are virgins to horror, just as we are virgins to voluptuousness]" (140). This perfectly described my unpreparedness in confronting this too quiet landscape, yet, I was curious enough to keep going through it. This curiosity, along with the sense of being uninitiated, resonates with the silence of Hadžhalilović's work, Maitland's unskinning, and my own discomfort in locations where silence may be extreme. Even for those who love and seek out silence, its texture can still take us unawares. Nothing prepares us for eerie silence, but its occurrence reinforces that silence does indeed have the capacity to work in radically different ways.

Maitland notes one of the problems with languages is that it is "... both the route to freedom and the route to 'good behaviour'" (2008: 54). Nowhere is this more in evidence than in Hogg's *Archipelago* where Patricia (Kate Fahy) must give voice to the reality of her marriage in order to move forward. For her, silence is "the route to good behaviour," and the intense landscape noise of the Scilly Isles gives her a perfect excuse for not using language to express her situation until it can no longer be concealed. Patricia's silence on certain topics is important as it displays the ways in which she is forgotten and under-appreciated, and how she cannot find the courage to use language as a route to freedom until her final confrontation with her husband over the phone.

Michelsen Foy's book chronicles his devotion to an ideal of "absolute silence." He becomes obsessed with noise levels in daily life and begins taking decibel measurements everywhere he goes. These measurements, combined with extensive research into environmental health policy, fuel his investigation into the tangible benefits of silence and his desire to relocate from New York City. Like Maitland, he is driven by a greater desire for silence and quiet in everyday life. Foy is conscious of his anomalous position, and documents the disagreements he has with his wife Liz about a proposed move to a quieter, and more spacious home. While some of his observations resonate with views expressed by both Prochnik and Maitland, Foy comes off as the writer who is perhaps most opposed to certain types of noise that characterize modern urban life and which are particularly difficult to minimize.

Prochnik is more practical in his search for silence, claiming "wherever you live there are ways of finding silence" (116) but this must be approached with care and dedication. Prochnik relates his own quest to locate "oases of silence" (116) in mid-town Manhattan, describing a series of small parks, art museums, and churches as places that can be sought out for those craving silence in cities. While Prochnik's thoughts are compelling, there is nothing particularly earth-shattering in his suggestion that those seeking quiet should look no further than their local library. There is a certain urban smugness to Prochnik's work that recalls Bigunet's assertions about silence as a marker of luxury. While Prochnik seeks out places which do not always charge admission to enter, there is a certainly an affluent quality to their Manhattan location, where money can be used to (quite literally) insulate oneself from a certain amount of unwanted noise. There is also a certain irony to seeking out pools of silence in highly urban locations, particularly in New York with its reputation as "the city that never sleeps." Prochnik's pursuit, not unlike Foy, seems to be about a kind of demand to have the world re-made around him. In contrast, Maitland acknowledges that in order to really obtain silence, one has to go to a location where deeper and more prolonged silence is physically possible and she does this by making herself a new home in a remote corner of Scotland. She too remakes the world around her, but she does not expect this to happen without significant effort and investment on her part. Maitland is prepared to change her way of living in order to obtain more silence. Michelsen Foy also moves to a quieter, more rural location in order to obtain silence. Prochnik simply wants the city to be quieter, without having to change anything about his own environment or way of living. All these writers advocate for silence as an aspect of wellness (as does Patrick Shen's documentary *In Pursuit of Silence*), but only Prochnik wants a quieter city. This question of how one wishes to experience silence is one that seems to change over the course of one's life, and fits in with the way *Quiet Pictures* is structured to examine women protagonists at different stages of their lives and the way the films themselves deploy silence as part of the narrative.

Stuart Sim's *A Manifesto for Silence* advocates from a scholarly perspective what Sara Maitland puts into practice: "Just as there is a politics of noise, so there can and should be a politics of silence" (2). But Sim is also careful to note that not everyone has access to the choices taken by writers like Maitland, Prochnik, and Michelsen Foy—the ability to downsize or retreat from urban noise "is not an option most can exercise it is essentially a middle-class, Western solution of limited capability" (5). Yet, increasingly we are all being advised that some silence is good for us. To be in silence, and to practice periods of silence and quietude are noted as valuable techniques of radical self-care. In Shen's *In Pursuit of Silence*, we witness the benefits of forest therapy in Japan, where studies have confirmed the substantial health benefits of spending time being quiet in nature.

The cinema itself remains a space (often a space located in a city) where the audience's silence is desired and mobile phone use is strongly discouraged. And yet, when it comes to certain kinds of filmmaking, we must account for the possibility of being confronted with textures and atmospheres of silence that are anything but restful, just as certain kinds of films tend to evoke verbal and bodily responses from viewers, forcing us to break the convention of the silent audience. These books and Shen's documentary constitute a groundswell of popular interest in silence. It is perhaps then less surprising that the work of these four directors explores different forms of silence. But further study of their work is therefore both necessary and timely, particularly as these films act as spaces where silence can be created and sustained.[2]

Women and Silence

A number of scholars have explored the significance of silence in relation to cinema and other performance contexts. What I want to do here is to draw together some of their ideas to formulate an approach to how silence works across these films, and how it acts as a distinct container for powerful thoughts, emotions, and gestures, to suggest that these films constitute a new cinema of silence. E. Ann Kaplan's work on women's silence in films by Marguerite Duras and others suggests that silence has a kind of power, much like that of silent protest. This idea also haunts Maitland's work where she discusses a letter she receives from a friend who is angry about Maitland's desire and quest for silence. Maitland's friend states that all silence is just waiting to be broken

---

[2] Other filmmakers also make substantive use of silence. The American filmmaker Kelly Reichardt has consistently deployed silence in her work. The British filmmaker William Oldroyd also deploys various textures of silence in his film *Lady Macbeth* (2017).

(Maitland 2008: 28). Maitland disagrees and sets out to argue for the political and personal worth of silence.

Vogelin's book *Listening to Noise and Silence* expresses ideas that are similarly resonant with Maitland and Kaplan; she notes, "The understanding of the self, born out of silence, politicizes the process of listening and the sonic subjectivity" (95). This suggests that silence can function as a radical space, and art that deploys silence can provide that space to the engaged spectator. Vogelin also reminds us that "silence is not the space left by sound but the space at the basis of all sound" (98). Silence is the thing that is always there, always with us. To strip our environment back to silence may be a way of priming the canvas, or clearing a work space from which new ideas can emerge. In *Morvern Callar,* Morvern praises "quiet places" and the idea of writing as a "slow" profession where you can "knock off when you want to ... smoke a cigarette, take a shower" and the audience is aware of how this differs considerably from her shift work in the supermarket. Allowed access to silence and solo travel, Morvern reinvents herself as an artist who is finally in control of her own surroundings.

Silence is something we can feel, as well as something we can engage in deliberately. Deliberate silence can be politically charged, and it can speak when words fail.[3] Vogelin argues that "silence is an experiential field as well as an ideological positioning" (99). Silence is, of course, also an accusation, especially when it concerns remaining silent in the face of repeated injustice. Yet, many people have also turned away from confronting the daily onslaught of horror, making liberal use of social media's ability to mute or block accounts, conversations, terms, and hashtags. This too is a deliberate silencing, an effort to control one's individual environment. We may no longer be virgins to horror, but we still implement silence as a kind psychological buffer against the traumatic onslaught of too much information. While caution and better management of one's personal digital footprint are in everyone's interest, it's not yet clear what the consequences of the falling silence of users abandoning various platforms might be. Silence is also a response—the unread, the

---

[3] Emma Gonzalez's speech and her deliberate use of timed silence at March for Our Lives, March 2018, https://www.theatlantic.com/entertainment/archive/2018/03/the-powerful-silence-of-the-march-for-our-lives/556469/

unanswered, the ignored, the awkward interaction for which one cannot find a suitable closure. To deliberately go silent may mean choosing not to comment, not to engage with a specific issue or individual. Silence can be deliberate or accidental in the context of our digital interactions.

"Respect your legends":[4] Marleen Gorris's *A Question of Silence* (1982) and Moufida Tlatli's *The Silences of the Palace* (1994)

Two of the most well-known examples of powerful on-screen silence that do anything but evoke the cliché of the ineffable are Marleen Gorris's *De stilte rond Christine M/A Question of Silence* (1982) and Moufida Tlatli's *Samt al qusur/The Silences of the Palace* (1994). In both these films, violence takes place silently, largely off screen, and acts of violence, complicity, and guilt are characterized by a refusal to speak.

In *A Question of Silence*, three strangers—a housewife, a waitress, and a secretary—murder a male shopkeeper in broad daylight. Christine (Edda Barends) the put-upon housewife is silently confronted by the male shopkeeper when he sees her stealing a dress. Rather than sheepishly returning the item, she stares into his face and boldly puts another item into her bag. Andrea (Henriëtte Tol) the secretary spots this and does the same, followed by Annie (Nelly Frijda), the waitress. Something about Christine's gesture galvanizes the other two—her silent defiance is contagious. The shopkeeper realizes he's outnumbered, as Christine, Andrea, and Annie move toward him and begin beating him. His killing takes place below the edge of the frame, so we never see his body, nor do we hear him cry out. The absence of the expected soundscape here (overlaid by an electronic score that would not be out of place in a giallo) is part of what makes this scene so strange and unsettling.

Linda Williams, writing about *A Question of Silence*, draws on the work of Elaine Showalter and others to suggest that the film, through its forms of silence, attempts to show us "a 'wild zone' or 'no-man's-land' of woman's culture that is

---

[4] This phrase is taken from Niven Govinden's novel *This Brutal House* (2019).

entirely off limits to men" (1994: 432). In this film, we encounter several forms of silence: as an absence of sound, an absence of speech, and silent, shared gazes between women. An absence of speech and shared gazes are readily apparent in the murder scene, where Christine, Andrea, and Annie converge to beat and mutilate the shop owner, while three other women silently look on. Later, during the trial these same three silent witnesses appear in the audience. Williams notes: "The violence of the crime and the negative disruption of laughter in the courtroom are their only forms of speech" (437) signaling that although the film contains dialogue, it is the conspicuous stretches of silence, and the disruptive laughter begun by the three accused women, that constitutes significant alternative forms of being heard and being seen. Williams also describes Christine's silence as "eerie" (435), since she refuses to speak for a long time after the killing, and when she does speak, it is to tell the psychiatrist to remind her husband of something, as if nothing untoward has occurred and she is still juggling the mental load of domestic life. Williams concludes her piece with the following statement:

> The power of *A Question of Silence* as feminist art thus lies in its resistance to all the male paradigms by which female deviance has been understood, in its insistence on the wildness of women's cultural experience and, finally, in its refusal to narrate the positive, utopian identity of women.
>
> (439)

This refusal to offer up a positive identity is connected to some of the ideas I wish to explore in *Quiet Pictures*. One of the ways silence is deployed in the work of these four directors is as a space for suggesting new identities, some of which are utopian (in the case of *Morvern Callar* and *Exhibition*) while others are far more troubling (as in *Evolution*, or *We Need to Talk About Kevin*).

In *The Silences of the Palace*, silence contains the never openly discussed sexual violence and sexual arrangements performed by the serving women of the Tunisian royal palace. This culminates in a powerful scene where the young protagonist Alia rushes to the locked palace gates and performs a silent scream (see Figure 1).

Figure 1 Alia's (Hend Sabry) silent scream at the gates of the palace in *Samt al-qusur/ The Silences of the Palace* (Moufida Tlatli, 1994).

This silent scream[5] acts as an example of what Justin Horton terms "abandoned sound":

> Perhaps the rarest of the deviations from sound cinema norms, abandoned sound is when all sounds—dialogue, direct sound, music, voice-over—are completely removed from the film, leaving the perceiver in a purely visual mode, as a spectator proper ... Abandoned sound is, therefore, a radical strategy, for it places the spectator in a position of silence that even the supposedly silent cinema did not ... In this regard, abandoned sound closely aligns with the category of intentional silence.
>
> (Horton 2013: 20)

This memorable sequence from *The Silences of the Palace* is a clear example of powerful, intentional silence, though it is markedly different from the powerful silences of Gorris's film. All elements of the soundtrack are abandoned in order to emphasize the plight of Alia and her compatriots, and to reinforce Alia as a profoundly conflicted figure who wishes to cry out, to express her anguish, and to flee the palace, but who also longs to remain close to the community

---

[5] The motif of the silent scream has a long history across other media, notably Edvard Munch's much re-produced painting *Skrik/The Scream* (1893), and in work such as Bertolt Brecht's *Mother Courage* (1939). I am grateful to David Pellegrini for reminding me about other occurrences of this motif.

of women she loves. Here, the physical anguish of the body's performance is the focus, as we realize that Alia has nowhere to run, and nowhere to scream. Alia's moving singing later in the film fulfills something similar to the disruptive laughter in *A Question of Silence*, since Alia's performance ruptures the atmosphere of a conservative party, just as the womens' laughter disrupts the courtroom.

Kaplan also writes about silence as a technique that can successfully express conflict and ambivalence, as it does in *A Question of Silence* and *The Silences of the Palace*. Focusing on the film work of Duras and Sontag, Kaplan notes that "for her [Duras] women's silence and passivity had a force ... " (2009: 163). Kaplan notes that for Sontag silence was an important idea, not only in relation to her well-known essay "The Aesthetics of Silence," but in terms of popular feminist discourse:

> A common trope in 1970s U.S. feminist theory ... was that of women (read white Western women) silenced in patriarchy. Feminists urged women to reject being silenced and to speak in their own voices. ... Some feminists saw silence as a possible form of resistance to patriarchy, empowering in its own right ... [Susan Sontag] saw silence as in part resistance to pain, a way to prevent further hurt, silence as offering complexity, nuance, depth in human interaction.
>
> (Kaplan 2009: 164)

This resonates with some of the many popular associations with silence as an act that has consequences, but this also acknowledges that silence is multifaceted and may be deployed as such. Silence can emerge as a form and technique of resistance.

Director Mike Figgis on being told that it is not possible to have total silence in a film remarks: "If you want silence, you have to have approximate silence with what's called 'room tone'. It's like quiet white noise. But you can't have zero" (Figgis 2003: 1). When Figgis is finally able to deploy total silence in a particular sequence in his film *Leaving Las Vegas*, he revels in the discomfort that occurs:

> And suddenly it's so quiet in the cinema that you can literally hear everything, and you don't have the protection of this sound blanket of mush, or just

ambient noise, or whatever, which we come to expect of a soundtrack. And I loved it. I thought that was exactly what I wanted, but it was even much more powerful than I thought it would be in my imagination.

(2003: 2)

These instances of powerful silence in *A Question of Silence* and *The Silences of the Palace*, and as described by Figgis are just some examples of the potential textures and impacts of silence. They indicate that there is much to examine when it comes to the ways in which silence is deployed in the cinema.[6]

All these filmmakers show us that silence can be powerful. Linda Dittmar asserts that in the cinema

> ... *silence can indeed be a positive value* [my emphasis]. As feminist cinemas of the 1970s and 1980s show, silence can also be oppositional. It can signal a holding of oneself apart, a resistance that cherishes one's inviolability. When emphasised, it can displace conventional notions of audibility and fluency and encourage audiences to listen in new ways and discover new, *hitherto unsuspected modes of eloquence and assertion* [my emphasis].
>
> (1994: 393–4)

It is this positive valuing of silence, and its ability to foster new ways of looking and being that I wish to explore in *Quiet Pictures*. Paul Théberge notes that "on the one hand, silence is valued as a form of tranquillity, and, on the other, it is often a sign of abnormality, something to be feared" (52). The use of silence and quietude in the cinema has a number of parameters that have been noted by scholars in the field of sound studies; it is only relatively recent developments in audio technology that permit quietude and near silence as an element of sound design, and that too much silence may be read by the audience as "a technical breakdown" (52). Silence as a key aspect of creating suspense and surprise has also contributed to our sense of silence in the cinema as something uneasy.

Théberge usefully elaborates and refines our terminology for analyzing silence in the cinema:

---

[6] While beyond the scope of this work, there is also clearly work to be done with regard to audiences and their responses to silence.

> "Silence" is always relative and relational to sounds heard in the context of the film itself. Relative degrees of silence have been used for specific effects in cinema for many years: for example, the general level of environmental noises can be attenuated, allowing for a focus on a particular sound ... or ambient sounds can be suppressed entirely, thus giving the impression of entering into the mind of a character. With regards to the latter, we can see that selected *parts* of the soundtrack that are silenced (producing, in this case, what might be referred to as a "diegetic silence"), whereas other parts such as music continue to sound or are given special prominence.
>
> (53–4)

Here, Théberge articulates a range of what we might term textures of silence, noting the various ways in which individual sounds can be isolated on the soundtrack through choices in sound design, giving an impression of the quietude or focus associated with silence without actually producing total silence (an effect sound designers indicate is impossible and additionally, often too deeply unsettling for any length of time, not unlike the effect of the anechoic chamber). Additionally, Théberge indicates that sequences where silence is overlaid by music are part of how we may consider the deployment of silence, particularly a character's verbal silence:

> It is important to note that diegetic silences–silences that are then filled by music or other non-diegetic sounds–are used not only to represent the inner life of characters, their dreams, fantasies, or moments of mental anguish, but also occasionally, in a somewhat different fashion, to represent any moment in which reality exceeds our expectation, when the real becomes surreal.
>
> (57)

This conceptualization of sequences where silence is "filled" by other non-diegetic sounds is essential, as it opens up a greater range of ways of thinking about how silence is created and evoked on screen. Lynne Ramsay's work in particular makes frequent use of this technique; indeed, it is a substantial structuring concern in *Morvern Callar* and *You Were Never Really Here* (2017). That said, the absence of music as well as dialogue silences are equally important for Théberge, and he notes that both of these types of silences "tend to be disguised" (59) or go unnoticed. Recently, the video essay format has allowed scholars to focus on both of these types of silences in a deeply material way, placing them side by side and cataloguing their frequency through editing.[7] Video Essays like Paul Verdeure's "When Words Fail" and Yoann Casal's "Silence Is Golden" reveal that both musical and dialogue silences are being noticed and remarked upon by scholars in a new way. Just as new technologies permit a greater range of silences to be designed in cinema, scholars now have the tools at their disposal to analyze these techniques in far greater detail.

To return to Sontag's interest in the look versus the stare, and how it relates to questions of silence, we might consider this in relation to two of the films in question here. We might make the following division: characters in Sciamma's films look, and in Hadžhalilović's the characters stare. In Sciamma's films, her protagonists spend time examining other women and girls, largely in an attempt to understand how to enact femininity, but also to observe what it means to be feminine, and in many cases, because they are also attracted to femininity. In Hadžhalilović's *Innocence* and *Evolution*, there is a certain unwavering, disconcerting quality to the intensity of the stares accompanied by what might be an unnerving level of silence for some viewers. Her young protagonists witness events they don't fully comprehend, yet they stare so as to try and make sense of the world around them. This is part of the unsettling affect of Hadžhalilović's films—their deployment of silence is rarely comforting. In Joanna Hogg's work, chatter often contrasts with a character's periodic, deep silence and contemplative looking. In Hogg's films, the worlds of well-off English people are often filled with the kind of conversation that conceals and avoids the discussion of emotion. Hogg's films tend to conform to Sontag's observation: "How often the aesthetic of silence appears alongside a barely controlled abhorrence of void" (27). Characters in *Unrelated* and *Archipelago* generally seem to abhor a void, a silence in which deeper contemplation of the self and society might occur. In contrast, *Exhibition* revels in the silence necessary for its artist couple to produce work. Here, there is no fear of a void, but rather a reluctance to shatter silence and say too much, "when punctuated by long silences, words weigh more … when one talks less, one begins feeling

---

[7] See David Verdeure's "When Words Fail," https://www.fandor.com/keyframe/watch-when-words-fail [August 9, 2016]. Yoann Casals's "Silence Is Golden: The Quietness of Soderbergh," https://vimeo.com/192828474 [November 24, 2016].

more fully one's physical presence in a given space" (Sontag 20). It is perhaps unsurprising that the artist couple seem to value and cultivate a silence that is similar to the silent environments in Marina Abramović's *The Artist Is Present* and *512 Hours*.

More Than This: The Desiring Gaze, the Desiring Ear

I would like to suggest that some of the silences in these films make space for what I am calling the desiring gaze and the desiring ear that we can move beyond the binary of look and stare, or silence and noise. As noted above, discussions of sound design rather than music have tended to be comparatively rare in film studies until recently. Yet, there have been earlier advocates for what we might term attentive listening alongside reconceptualizations of the gaze.[8] Jack Halberstam writes about the relationship between sound and fear for women in horror cinema:

> Fear can also be produced from a sound: a click, a shutter (shudder?), "knocking." Productive fear, therefore, circulates through the power of the gaze but also through the power of directed listening. Within the structure of the horror film, furthermore, it is very often sound rather than sight that produces tension for the female viewer—soundtracks, for example, match and produce expected somatic responses to the images on the screen. … Very often the music transforms a spectator into a listener and then makes listening a part of the identifications between audience and victim or audience and slasher.
>
> (Halberstam 1995: 127)

If productive fear can come from the gaze and the ear, then why not productive desire? This productive desire might in turn produce a more collaborative gaze. Linda Williams in her landmark essay "Film Bodies: Gender, Genre, Excess" argues for horror, pornography, and melodrama as "body genres" but there is a similar correspondence at work in these films, where silences work in tandem

---

[8] Kathryn Lachman notes in her discussion of *Petite Maman*: "Sciamma has told interviewers that she sought to make spectators listen more attentively" (2023: 7).

with the body and its ability to look, stare, and gaze, its ability to listen, to speak or remain mute, its ability to make different kinds of noise. I would like to argue that these films want us to notice their silences and in turn the ways in which bodily gestures are contained within those silences.

In Sciamma's *Portrait of a Lady on Fire/Portrait de la jeune fille en feu*, we see many of the concerns I have enumerated here come to the fore. As Marianne (Noémie Merlant) and Héloïse (Adèle Haenel) begin to realize their desire for one another, it is the way they silently watch one another that gives this away. We notice their looks because of the silence. Of course, this is a story of an artist commissioned to make a portrait of an unwilling sitter, a model who will not consent to being painted because she knows it is a precursor to being married off. The betrothal portrait means an end to the relative freedom Héloïse has known as part of her convent education, and she has already defeated one artist prior to Marianne's arrival. Observing Héloïse by stealth, sketching in her free moments during their shore walks, and from memory Marianne creates the first portrait, a portrait that enrages Héloïse and which Marianne immediately defaces, rubbing out the face in the still wet pigment. It is only once Héloïse consents to be painted that desire is permitted to flourish and the subtle aspects of mutual gazing take place. This acknowledgment of the need for collaboration and consent is furthered by the dissolution of household hierarchies in the absence of Héloïse's mother during the five days allocated to the second portrait attempt. When the household servant Sophie (Luàna Bajrami) reveals her unwanted pregnancy, Marianne and Héloïse immediately begin to help and support her, encouraging her to engage in vigorous exercise, searching for abortifacient herbs, and they end by accompanying Sophie and caring for her after her visit to the local sage-femme. During this short period of time, a dynamic of equality is established between the three women, and we see them cooking, eating, drinking, playing cards, and enjoying each other's conversation. During one of the sessions where Héloïse poses for Marianne, they begin to reveal the ways in which each has been observing the other, her subtle gestures and moods. This is not the obsessive stare of the voyeur; this is the desiring gaze, the gaze that looks and looks back, the collaboration of mutual attraction. These are two women who have come to desire one another and some of the ways they have gained knowledge of the person who will become a lover are by observing and listening to their body: their breath, their glances. Rather than being a way of obtaining knowledge that is open only to the expert eye of the trained artist, this exchange too is part of the atmosphere of equality. Héloïse is not the passive object trapped in amber by the voyeur's stare; she is quite clearly in possession of a desiring gaze of her own, one that she offers to Marianne to return. This mutually desiring gaze is introduced when Marianne sketches the sleeping Héloïse, who then awakens and smiles at her, meeting Marianne's gaze. What might have otherwise been a voyeuristic stare is disrupted by the presence of a silent, but nonetheless welcoming, consenting gaze that is returned. The sequence of shots is important here—neither Marianne nor Héloïse looks directly into the camera, this is not the kind of sequence that places the viewer on top of the erotic object, but instead we are off to the side, still able to see their exchange of gazes and expressions clearly, and note the direction of their gazes toward one another. This all takes place in the build-up to the exchange of the first kiss between the lovers, establishing a visual language of desire that privileges equality, and acknowledges the best kind of collaborative relationship that can exist between an artist and model when consent is freely given.

After their conversation about how they have observed one another, both Marianne and Héloïse are unsettled by what their shared gaze has revealed.

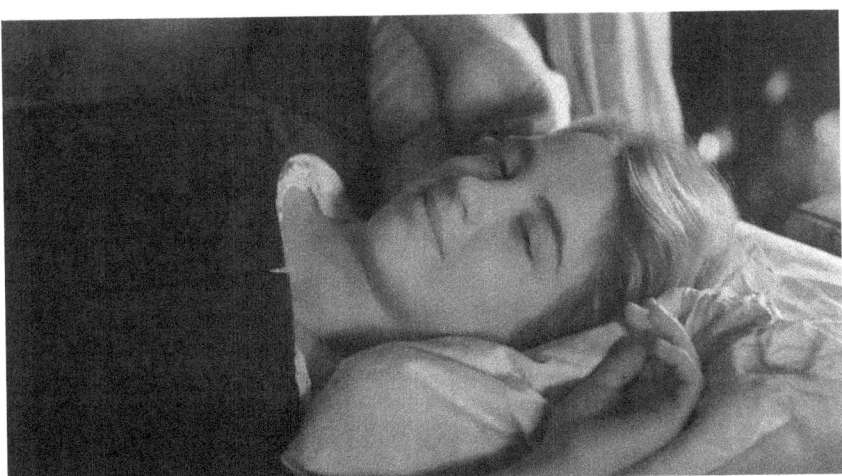

Figure 2 Héloïse (Adèle Haenel) gazes at Marianne.

Figure 3 Héloïse and Marianne gaze at one another, unsettled by desire.

Having acknowledged their intimate observations of each other's expressions and emotions ("When you're troubled, you breathe through your mouth," Héloïse tells Marianne) they are left with the possibility of what has been revealed, namely their desire for one another. This desire is communicated largely through the exchange of gazes, gestures, and embraces far more than it is through verbal exchange. The two images above (see Figures 2 and 3) from *Portrait of a Lady on Fire* are emblematic of the ways in which silence consistently contains a range of emotions in Sciamma's work: erotic tension, comfort, sensuality. Emma Wilson confirms this, noting that "Sciamma creates sensory worlds in her films, that are not only formally controlled but expressive, beyond language … [Sciamma's] films look at embodied existence, sensory life, gestures, emotions, silence and stillness" (Wilson 2021: 14). In *Portrait of a Lady on Fire*, as in many of the films under discussion here, language is no substitute for the silent sharing of a gaze, or the wordless gesture that gives agency.

In *King Kong Theory*, Virgine Despentes asks: "Why do mothers encourage little boys to be noisy, while little girls have to keep quiet?" (2006/2010: 115). This gendering of silence is also what concerns me in this book. These are films filled with rich and varied silences enacted by and around bodies, and many of those bodies are coded at one time or another as femme. The way in which silence and quietude work here is to turn the screen into a threshold, calling attention to the limitations frequently placed on the characters we encounter in terms of their bodies, gazes, and voices. As Legacy Russell remarks, "While we continue to navigate towards a more vast and abstract concept of gender, it must be said that it really does feel, paradoxically, as if all we have are the bodies we are housed in, gendered or otherwise. Under the sun of capitalism we truly own little else" (2020: 9). Certainly these films do suggest that the bodies we are housed in are limited by gendered expectations, and that many of these expectations are implicit, never clearly or fully articulated. In this scenario, silence can be harmful, oppressive, hard to overcome particularly for child and adolescent characters. But silence is also the space in which a look or a stare can become a shared gaze of understanding or attraction.

As Annie Ernaux via Alison Strayer's translation reminds us, "a body is breath—life and desire have no gender" (2022: 126).

Lose Yourself, Find Yourself: Anger, Desire, Risk, Loss, Aging

When Céline Sciamma's *Petite Maman* made its UK debut in October 2021, I was once more moved by the tender silences of her work and I was awed by how this film, a film made about mothers by someone who, like me, has chosen not to become a mother, fit into the larger project of this book. During the writing of this book, my beloved mother-in-law passed away very suddenly, and I became someone who had lost a mother. In *Petite Maman*, Sciamma explores those relationships that take us from cradle to grave.

The film begins with a word game being played between an elderly woman and the film's child protagonist Nelly (Josephine Sanz). It is slowly revealed that this woman is one of her grandmother's neighbors in the care home where she has just died. Nelly's mother Marion (Nina Meurisse) is clearing out her mother's room, before she, Nelly and Nelly's father (Stéphane Varupenne) drive to Marion's childhood home. There is melancholia here, and the fresh presence of grief, but it is grief perceived through the eyes of a child. Once they arrive at the house, Marion and her partner begin the task of clearing out the house, ridding it of books, furniture and other items. Nelly goes out into the woods, intent on trying to find the location of her mother's hut or "cabane," the wooden structure she built from a fortuitous placement of trees. The image of childhood on offer here is as pastoral as that of her earlier film *Tomboy*, and this woodland lacks the sinister edge of the spaces inhabited by Hadžhalilović's child protagonists. In *Innocence* and *Evolution*, nature is both controlled and controlling, another boundary place where children can play but from which they cannot escape. In Sciamma's films, nature is a place to be, but also a threshold space of becoming for many of her characters regardless of age. The exception to this is *Girlhood*, but even in that film airy, outdoor spaces are present—the square where girls perform dances for other girls, and the open space we can see in the frame that Vic runs out of at the end. Nevertheless, we can see that the relationship to space is different for the characters in *Girlhood* than in Sciamma's other films and this may well be part of the ways in which *Girlhood* has been re-evaluated as a film that does not do enough to advocate authentically for its Afropean protagonists.

When Nelly spots another girl in the woods dragging a huge branch, she greets her, and we discover the other girl is Marion (Gabrielle Sanz), the "petite maman" of the title. As Nelly follows Marion back to her house, we see the mirror world of the past, the same hall with its hidden cupboard and the same layout of rooms. As Nelly and Marion play together, we are treated to the tender idea of being able to know our parent throughout their entire life, and that this bond runs so deep that it can transcend time. When Nelly tells Marion she's her daughter, and Marion asks if she's from the future, Nelly simply replies "the path behind you" and shows her the twin house, where they go inside to greet Nelly's father. When the two girls have their sleepover in child Marion's house, Marion tells Nelly "I'm already thinking about you" knowing that she wanted to be a mother. *Petite Maman* presents a radically different vision of motherhood from the other films on offer here that deal with caregiving and maternity. Its title, in both French and its English translation "little mother," suggests a reappropriation of a term that is sometimes applied to young girls who behave with maturity toward their younger peers or siblings. Bianca (Bérangère Haubruge) in *Innocence* might well be described as a "little mother" to her younger classmates. Here, the title is literal, in the sense that Nelly encounters Marion as a child and as an adult, but it also suggests that the maternal itself can be small, quotidian, much more about play and the caring gestures we see between Nelly and both of her parents, as well as between Nelly and child Marion. This quiet but expansive image of the maternal could not be further from the ambivalent maternities of *We Need to Talk About Kevin* and *Evolution*. Instead, Sciamma presents us with a radical tenderness that extends across three generations, but particularly emphasizes the bond between mother and daughter.

When I began this book, I thought it was about silence in a rather technical sense. But I soon realized that silence is a quality and a texture that I had to define and appreciate more carefully. I also confronted the fact that total silence is a rarity in the cinema, and a lot of the time what I was really looking at were moments that eschewed dialogue or music, or where music filled up the silences where characters weren't able to speak. I also realized that silence was essentially the canvas which allowed the quality of a look or a gaze to emerge and to function in a different, and at times radically intimate way.

Then I thought about noise—all the noise of the things that happened while I was writing this book: the Trump presidency, Brexit, the Black Lives Matter protests, rising austerity, an enormous wave of transphobia in the UK, and the overturning of Roe vs. Wade (to name but a few). This was contrasted by the terrifying quiet of strict lockdown during the height of the Covid-19 pandemic, a period when I found it difficult to write.

When I found I was able to return to work on this book in a meaningful way in Autumn 2021, I suddenly saw what else I was writing about—the silence of taboo and how bodies speak to us and for us. There is a silence that is discernible here in these films and it mainly concerns anger and desire. In *We Need to Talk About Kevin*, Eva's (Tilda Swinton) rage and frustration cannot be articulated because to do so would be to explode the conventions of maternal care. Many of these conventions exist for good reasons—to protect children from harm, to sustain the kind of support structures that allow sustainable, "good enough" parenting to take place. And yet, the idea of regretting or hating motherhood is terrifying. And this is different from not wanting to become a mother and holding to that position. What is terrifying about Eva is that she does not want to be a mother after she sees her child, and this child goes on to commit an atrocity, an atrocity for which Eva feels responsible, and for which society holds her accountable. This stands in contrast to *Unrelated* and Anna's deep sense of loss at the occurrence of menopause, and the realization that she will no longer be able to become pregnant.

As much as this is a book about silence, it is also a book about loss, and how these filmmakers use silence to address our most profound losses, losses for which we struggle to find the appropriate words and gestures. Silence is one of the only responses Morvern can offer when faced with her partner's suicide. In the silence of Samantha Morton's low-dialogue performance, we see the flailing gestures of a someone who does not quite know how to find the words to say what has happened, but who can still make meaningful bodily gestures that eventually take her into a new kind of life. In the silence of the empty flat Morvern dismembers her lover, finding solace in listening to *The Velvet Underground*'s "I'm Stickin' with You." Throughout *Morvern Callar*, music fills up uncomfortable silences and creates a kind of sonic bubble around Morvern that allows her to mourn in her own way. Sex with other people also fills up the emptiness, the silence: at the party near the start of the film, in the resort hotel in Spain, Morvern finds bodily connection, and this continues as she dances, and moves into greater solitude traveling alone, without fear, into the unknown.

These are also films that deal with loss of first love. In *Water Lilies* and *Girlhood*, Marie (Pauline Acquart) and Marieme/Vic (Karidja Touré) both experience longing and loss. Marie longs for Floriane (Adèle Haenel), and her friend Anne (Louise Blachère) longs for François (Warren Jacquin), but more than this, they both long to be seen in the sense of being fully noticed and perceived by their crushes. Both Marie and Anne experience physical encounters with their crushes, but eventually realize they have placed their hopes in people who cannot reciprocate, and what they find in the end is a sense of belonging in their friendships with one another. Floriane and François have served their purpose in terms of a realization of desire, but this is not the kind of film that concludes with happy teen couples. These are also films about adults losing and finding innocence: in *Unrelated* Anna experiences a period of freedom before seemingly returning to her ordinary life. She sees the choices that Verena and others have made to become parents, and while she may have regrets, she makes her peace with her own choices, as well as the events over which she has no control (such as the end of her fertility). In *Morvern Callar*, Morvern experiences a period of unfettered freedom, one that does not end with the film's conclusion.

All of these films deal at times in the body's plateaus of ardor and where those bodies might find connection—through place, dance, or sex. *Morvern Callar, Exhibition, Unrelated, Girlhood, Water Lilies, Portrait of a Lady on Fire, The Souvenir Part I* and *II*—all deal in desire and risk.

In *Unrelated*, the idea that Anna and Oakley (Tom Hiddleston) desire one another can be shown but it cannot be explicitly discussed, nor can it be fulfilled (at least in this narrative). To do this would be to explode the conventions of what is permitted to be desirable in heterosexual coupling under patriarchy. In pornography, this kind of desire between older and younger partners is not only permitted but fetishized, but rarely do we see it elsewhere in cinema except explicitly as a transgression, often between older men and younger women. In *Unrelated*, this flirtation is still transgressive, and it is clear that Anna and Oakley want something from each other, even if it is only the acknowledgment of being *seen*, and in that being seen, knowing that you are desired. In *Exhibition*, D's solo sexuality is rich and fascinating, in a way that feels revolutionary. But, I would also like to see this kind of mature, feminine sexuality depicted in relation to other bodies. This is not to accuse Hogg of not going far enough, but it is a call to arms for future filmmakers.

In *The Souvenir Part I* and *II* (2019 and 2021), we trace the experiences of Julie, Hogg's own avatar as embodied by Honor Swinton-Byrne. Through her relationship with the mysterious Anthony (Tom Burke), Julie is offered opportunities to take greater risks in her personal life, both in terms of how she navigates the relationship with Anthony and the influences he brings into her life. This combination of elation and risk is hinted at early in *The Souvenir Part I*, when Anthony and Julie first meet at a party at her flat. He appears as someone else's guest, and as she tells him about her film project to be set in Sunderland, we hear two songs as the undercurrent to their conversation: "Love My Way" by The Psychedelic Furs and "The Passion of Lovers" by Bauhaus. To note the presence of these songs, one must practice deliberate, attentive listening and attend to the music choices, the conversation dialogue, and the physical gestures and expressions of the two characters. Where the lyrics to "Love My Way" speak of a longing for fulfillment and following one's impulses, "The Passion of Lovers" suggests a dark, dangerous liaison. These two songs, released within a year of each other and emblematic of 1980s new wave and goth, carefully evoke the atmosphere of fascination that will characterize the relationship between Julie and Anthony. Julie and Anthony are compelling to one another but their relationship is strangely conventional, even sterile, until he writes to her from Paris declaring his love, and returns with a gift of a black garter belt and stockings. We don't see them embrace or kiss for a long time, though clearly further intimacies are imminent when he presents Julie with a pink parcel lying on the bed, which she opens in the bathroom before returning to the bedroom wearing the garter belt, to find him already naked under the covers. She climbs into bed, their foreheads nearly touching, before she lifts the quilt to cover herself as she begins to fellate him and Anthony groans, covering his face. Only after this does she find the track marks on his arm, a silent revelation of his heroin use. One of the only other times we see these lovers embracing is during the silent, ritualistic sex they have together in Venice—a place filled with their silences about Anthony's lack of ready money, but where fleeting experiences of luxury and sensuality are shown and experienced, with Julie wearing a custom-tailored suit Anthony has had made for her, as well as a magnificent pale gray ballgown that she wears to La Fenice. Under these highly feminine garments lies the garter belt, the object that allows these two lovers to unlock their sexual feelings for one another and express them through gestures.

It is only after Anthony's death that Julie is able to conceive and complete her graduation film, and she finds herself abandoning her early plans for the Sunderland project, in favor of a film that is more personal. Early on in *The Souvenir Part II* Julie is offered some apt but seemingly throwaway advice from arrogant fellow director Patrick (Richard Ayoade) who tells her "make a memorial for him [Anthony]" and this is indeed what Julie does, against the advice and wishes of her film school instructors. Through therapy, where she is able to access and confront her own difficult emotions, Julie comes to realize that, just as Audre Lorde tells us, her silence will not protect her from being hurt or from risk. With this in mind, she builds her graduation film on Anthony's silence and absence.[9] Anthony's death is painful and sudden,

---

[9] In *I Love Dick*, Chris Kraus writes of Dick "your sexy, cryptic silence, the silence that I'd written on" (128). There is something of that in *The Souvenir Part II* as well, where Julie's creative voice floods into the silence Anthony leaves behind.

but it also frees her creatively and sexually. We see evidence of this when she goes to Patrick's set to reconnect with her film school peers after taking time off to mourn. While there, she exchanges silent but powerful gazes with Jim, one of the actors (Charlie Heaton) who later turns up unannounced and late at night at her flat (a booty call avant la lettre, if you will). Jim is confident, entirely aware of his own striking appeal and Heaton gives him both swagger and charm. He appears through the spyhole of the flat door, in an oversize snake-print jacket, and the creak of the leather fills in the silences between his questions to Julie as he stands in her doorway: "Can I come in? … Are you okay? Are you sure?" Julie opens the door to him in white silk pyjamas, staring, subtly nodding in response to this gorgeous person who has appeared with such impeccable timing. Julie doesn't speak, but as Jim moves toward her they start kissing, and their mutual desire is evident by the way they grasp each other, and the sound of their sharp, rapid breathing (see Figure 4).

Figure 4 Julie (Honor Swinton-Byrne) and Jim (Charlie Heaton) make out in *The Souvenir Part II*.

After a moment or two, she very quietly tells him "stop, stop. I have my period" to which he nods and then replies, entirely unfazed, "I don't mind." As they hastily remove their trousers to fuck on the bed, Hogg's camera reveals Jim watching himself in the mirror. Afterwards, he goes down on Julie, and then kisses her, leaving her mouth smeared with her own menstrual blood. She watches him leave, and he silently looks her up and down before stepping into the elevator. Jim's once-over look seems a calculated move, part of his arsenal of seduction as he delivers this glance over the turned-up collar of his snake print jacket. This glance recalls Anthony's remark in *The Souvenir Part I* "You're a dark horse, Julie" as she goes to fellate him after putting on the garter belt. Where Anthony remains a distant, unknowable, sophisticated junkie, there is something decidedly rougher and less posh about Jim, a departure from the slightly more aloof sexiness of Tom Burke's Anthony or Tom Hiddleston's Oakley in *Unrelated*. Hogg films this moment of Jim's assessing glance from just behind Julie's shoulder, so both lovers are in the frame, and we are conscious of witnessing how Julie is positioned in relation to Jim's silent look, that she returns his look, and that the gaze here is shared between them in a way that bears some resemblance to the shared gazes between Marianne and Héloïse in *Portrait of a Lady on Fire*. This too is an instance of silent collaboration and desire. After he leaves, Julie returns to her bedroom and looks down at the blood-stained sheet. This sequence is presented not as a source of shame for Julie, but as an experience, an attempt at seizing on and exploring an opportunity, of acting on a desire that is mutual but that is never really articulated verbally. This in itself is not unusual, since so much on-screen sex takes place without dialogue, but what is significant here is the depiction of a casual sexual encounter taken up by a young, female protagonist who is not later punished for her decision, a decision that is not without risk. This encounter marks a turning point for Julie, as we see her begin to embrace both risk and desire on her own terms.

In *Portrait of a Lady on Fire*, desire and risk are also intertwined. When Héloïse and Marianne acknowledge their desire for one another, Héloïse is afraid but it is desire that silently propels her into Marianne's chamber. As they lie in bed together, Héloïse offers up the mysterious paste that let's one "fly" and prolong time, which she suggests they try together. This too is a risk, but one that is portrayed as pleasurable, making space for a silent sensuality focused on the lips and the armpit. Eschewing expectations, Sciamma neither focuses on displaying genitalia in a way that is expected in pornography, nor does she favor the torso bucking with the force of orgasm[10] so beloved of the explicit art film. This sequence constitutes a more experimental approach to queer bodily pleasure by focusing on the erotic possibilities of the armpit.[11] That said, it is vital to acknowledge that silence-as-absence can also be a problem, and the decision not to show the parts of the body that are conventionally involved in sexual intercourse can sometimes feel like censorship.[12] A strong sense of a double standard remains in place when we consider how femme bodies are shown on screen nude, or in various states of arousal. Sciamma's careful depictions in *Portrait of a Lady on Fire* and elsewhere remind us that we often see femme bodies as automatically exploited and without agency. There is still a sense that masculine bodies can appear on screen nude, and even in a state of arousal, without surrendering their autonomy. Michèle Bacholle argues that "Sciamma respects the women's intimacy as sex always occurs off screen, but toys with her viewers' conditioning to male-gaze in a close-up scene that presents two fingers entering a slit that turns out to be the fold of Héloïse's armpit 'penetrated' by Marianne." (2022: 1) And yet, it does rather depend on whether one categorizes this gesture as a form of sex. Certainly, Sciamma keeps anything that resembles conventional sex acts off screen here, but the focus on the armpit suggests that we can trust this is more than a joke, more than just toying with the viewer's conditioning. Like the silences in her films that contain multitudes, this gesture in itself suggests there are more plateaus of bodily ardor to be explored.

---

[10] This motif of the bucking torso can be seen in a range of films including the controversial *Blue Is the Warmest Colour* (Abdellatif Kechiche, 2013), *The Handmaiden* (Park Chan-wook, 2016), and *Ammonite* (Francis Lee, 2020). More unusual depictions of lesbian sexuality can be found in Rose Troche's *Go Fish* (1994) and Campbell X's *Stud Life* (2010).

[11] While the armpit has long been a body part appreciated by queer men, a similar appreciation has not always been evident in cinema that depicts women who have sex with women. Some of the photographs produced by Barbara Hammer in the 1970s offer an indication that this body part has come in for appreciation in terms of a lesbian eroticism (see pp. 48–9 "Bowsprit, Hornby Island British Columbia, 1972," in Hammer's *Truant: Photographs 1970–1979*).

[12] Films such as *Theo and Hugo/Théo et Hugo dans le même bateau* (Olivier Ducastel and Jacques Martineau, 2016) take a more open approach, offering explicit depictions of physical arousal and full frontal nudity without fanfare.

Water/Liquid/Fluid

Water features in all of Joanna Hogg's films: in *Archipelago* we are on the Scilly Isles, surrounded by water. In *Unrelated*, there are swimming pools but also the sweat of Italy in high summer, and the sweat of bodies in intimacy. In *Exhibition*, there are pools, naked swimming, and solo sexuality. In Ramsay's *Morvern Callar*, there's the bath Morvern and Lanna (Kathleen McDermott) take together after the party, the weird and humiliating pool games in Spain, and the sensuous solo showers Morvern takes after returning from the clubs. There is also the bathtub as the place where Morvern bathes, mourns, cries, and where she dismembers the body of her lover—it is the place where she cleanses herself and commits her last act of devotion to James. In *Evolution*, the ocean is a force, where Nicolas (Max Brebant) and his maternal captors swim, but there is also the suggestion of the ocean as an unknown realm that can entrap or nourish. Sciamma's *Water Lilies* is all about pools and their sensuous possibilities—a site of eroticism, of display, of competitive athleticism and femininity. In *Tomboy*, the bath is the site where Laure/Mikaël (Zoé Héran) gender trouble is revealed to the viewer and the bathroom is a site of transformation, along with the bedroom mirror, the place where Laure/Mikäel creates a phallus for themselves ahead of a trip to swim in a lake. Laure/Mikäel engages in this act to successfully manage their body, to present in the way that feels right. In *Girlhood*, Lady (Assa Sylla) calls Marieme into the hotel room bathroom. As Lady lounges in the bath, she bestows on Marieme important advice for life, and christens her with a new, gender-neutral name: Vic. Even though it is "Vic, come Victoire," Vic keeps this name as they pursue a more non-conforming gender expression. In all these films, water and mirrors are sites of transformation. These reflecting places are also, quite often, private or semi-private spaces, spaces of intimacy concerned with cleanliness, hygiene, but also with concealing the body's functions from others. To invite another person into these spaces is to bestow and share intimacy, to share or reveal transformation. In *We Need to Talk About Kevin*, the bathroom sink is the liminal space that reveals mother and son as twin beings, as irrevocably connected, their faces blurring into one another. The sprinkler is the soft, watery sound that leads Eva outside to discover her husband and daughter shot through with arrows on the back lawn. Kevin is conceived on a rainy night, as Eva and Franklin cavort ecstatically in a rain-slicked city before engaging in unprotected sex. In Hogg's *The Souvenir Part I*, the lovers go to Venice, and it is only in Venice that they become sensual with one another, as if gray and overcast London cannot allow them to fully express and explore their physical desires. In *Portrait of a Lady on Fire* we are by the sea again, buffeted by strong winds like the characters in *Archipelago*. In *Portrait*, this kingdom of women is like a jewel, where mirrors once more play a role, in the intimate sketch Marianne makes of Héloïse, holding a round mirror over her vulva, concealing that opening to show the face of her lover, the artist, as she makes work. There is also the portrait making as mirror, and the way what happens to art supplies is important. Paint, and specifically oil paint, is a wet medium, hydrophobic, and taking a long time to dry, to remain permanent. In amongst all this is for many of the characters except the very young, the fluids of the body: blood, cum, sweat, and saliva. These "waters" also make appearances in many of the films. The body does not always make noise: often menstrual blood is silent, but these other secretions are often accompanied by sound, especially on screen—the sound of a sweating body, a swimming body, a body exerting itself in the sun or during sex, the sound of orgasm, the sound of a kiss, the sound of flesh being wounded.

Death/Euphoria/Men

What no one tells you is that after loss sometimes comes bliss or euphoria. This is what Julie in *The Souvenir Part II* experiences when she completes her film and embarks on an exciting career. The presence of Anna Calvi's thrumming, rising song "Drive" on the soundtrack, is emblematic of this force for joy and excitement, which culminates in the film's final moments of quiet, as the camera moves out of the sounds of Julie's birthday party and into the sound stage where filming is taking place, with Hogg's crew positioned in the darkness. When Hogg's voice authoritatively calls "cut," the finality of this single word suggests a sense of confidence and accomplishment, aligned with Julie's own success. The final moments of Lynne Ramsay's *Morvern Callar* evoke a feeling of being alone with one's own thoughts, while also feeling held by a crowd of fellow dancers and the music you choose for yourself. This too can be seen to evoke a sense of accomplishment or achievement, because Morvern has managed to change her life and to seize autonomy from events which have happened *to* her. Like Julie, she too has suffered a sudden bereavement, a thing that has come at her out of nowhere where she must deal with the consequences. Both James and Anthony leave silence in their wake—their deaths have causes, but what ultimately drives each of them toward an early death remains opaque. Theirs is the silence out of which Morvern and Julie become their authentic selves. This contrasts with the ways in which silent, absent men haunt the narratives of both *Unrelated* and *Archipelago*, the way their phone calls intrude on the holiday, and how both Anna and Patricia remain tethered to their unseen men, the difficulties of their marriages "dissolving into silence" as Joanna Walsh says of successful marriages, with arguments and tensions seemingly ignored or forgotten. Men fare somewhat better in Sciamma's films particularly in paternal roles, with the tender, communicative, and sympathetic fathers of *Tomboy* (Mathieu Demy) and *Petite Maman* (Stéphane Varupenne). In *Water Lilies*, men are either distant objects of adoration or predators, the crush or the older men who proposition Floriane. In *Girlhood*, men are a distinct threat to Marieme/Vic's autonomy, particularly their brother Djibril (Cyril Mendy) and the crime boss Abou (Djibril Gueye), both of whom bring judgment and the threat of violence. In *Portrait of a Lady on Fire* men barely appear at all. In Sciamma's *Portrait*, as in Joanna Hogg's first two films, there is also a sense of being silently haunted by a male presence: there is the specter of the heterosexual marriage Héloïse must make, and there is Sophie's unwanted pregnancy. While we only ever see men on screen peripherally, the way in which they shape the fates of these women is always at the edges.

In addition to these various themes, this book is structured into chapters that deal with roles or life stages: childhood, adolescence, motherhood, the artist-exhibitionist, and age. Chapter 1 focuses on childhood and the ways in which Hadžhalilović's *Innocence* and *Evolution* alongside Sciamma's *Tomboy* make space for the development of a child gaze via techniques of silence. Instances of prolonged looks, and silence in the form of things that remain unspoken, are what characterize these three films that focus on girls, boys, and the gender fluid Laure/Mikaël of *Tomboy*. Chapter 2 deals with adolescence and motifs of coming-of-age and gender expression in Sciamma's *Water Lilies* and *Girlhood*, and the ways in which silence in the form of direct and indirect gazes focalizes fragile and tender interactions between friends and lovers. Chapter 3 deals in largely sinister and ambivalent images of motherhood in Ramsay's *We Need to Talk About Kevin* and the figures I have called the "Not Mothers" of Hadžhalilović's *Evolution*. Chapter 4 formulates the figure of the Artist-Exhibitionist, taking up the figure of women who embark on narratives of erotic and artistic experimentation, in Ramsay's masterpiece *Morvern Callar* and Joanna Hogg's *Exhibition*, contextualizing these two figures in relation to the earlier flâneuse figure in art and literature. This chapter explores how silence becomes a tool of transformation in the hands of Morvern and D, who both fashion their artistic selves out of silence, alongside a mature individuality. Chapter 5 focuses premdominantly on two of Joanna Hogg's films: *Unrelated* and *Archipelago*, and how silence works to hem in women in late middle age. This chapter also explores what it would mean to unpack some of the taboos around marital satisfaction, sexuality, and eroticism that have tended to characterize the portayal of middle-aged women in the cinema. The book concludes with a brief consideration of the importance of crafting a collaborative gaze through the deliberate deployment of forms of silence, and what it means to know how to use your gaze.

1

Childhood, Curiosity, and Compliance in *Innocence, Evolution*, and *Tomboy*

In *Innocence, Evolution*, and *Tomboy* Hadžhalilović and Sciamma deploy silence as a place to develop the child gaze as a way of representing what Sara Ahmed calls "emergent personhood." Of her own childhood and adolescence, Ahmed remarks of the prevalence of her encounter with the term "tomboy" which Sciamma deploys as the title of her film:

> In my late teens I was regularly called a tom-boy, although looking back, I was just a girl not that interested in being girly, in dresses, or makeup, or talking about boys. … That a not-girly girl is called a tomboy teaches us how restricted *girl* can be as a category of emergent personhood.
>
> (2017: 53)

This sense of girl as a restricted category is present in *Innocence*, while the exploration of tomboy as a category or identity is part of what defines Sciamma's film. In both films, the child gaze is perceptive, comprised of exploring thresholds and other places of becoming, as well as silence as a space of holding. Characters here are raised as girls, as boys, and somewhere in between. While Hadžhalilović's work deals with how children navigate scenarios that are uncanny and sinister, Sciamma offers up a deeply moving portrait of how a single character navigates and explores gender at a stage when they do not really have the words to articulate their feelings and desires.

Both *Innocence* and *Evolution* begin with water, its sounds, and currents. In both films, bodies of water suggest a world that is sealed off from elsewhere, and water acts as a threshold for these child protagonists, who are not physically strong enough to cross the barrier without help. In *Innocence*, a girl tries to row her way out of the park that surrounds the school and is never seen again. In *Evolution*, Nicolas (Max Brebant) can only escape the island with help from Stella (Roxane Duran). Crucially, we also see child protagonists abandoned in water at the end of each film, with Nicolas alone in a small boat, offshore from a refinery and in *Innocence*, Bianca (Bérangère Haubruge) wades into a fountain, where she sees a boy for the first time. As Matilda Mroz notes in the case of *Innocence*, "the hermetically enclosed school grounds can be seen as a kind of aquarium in which the girls play in water and on land, and which the camera at times observes via what [Emma] Wilson has termed a 'surveillant mode', that 'view[s] little girls from above and afar, as an entomologist observes a colony of ants'" (2007: 176 quoted in Mroz, 2016: 288). The implications of this surveillant mode are significant in terms of how it positions an adult look or stare as separate from the child gaze, tapping into an anxiety that Vicky Lebeau describes as being "not only about what adults *do* to children, but *how they look at them*" (Lebeau, 2008: 120). In *Evolution*, adults are quite literally alien beings who appear to care for the boys on the island, but who also experiment on their bodies. In *Innocence*, the teachers survey the girls for proper behavior. In Hadžhalilović's first two feature films children are kept in secluded landscapes, and in a state of seeming ignorance of which they grow increasingly suspicious. This sense of suspicion is maintained in *Earwig*, though the setting is even more claustrophobic and isolated, since much of the film takes place indoors.

Innocence begins with quiet, and the deliberately strange site of a small coffin with a mesh window carried by unseen hands lends the narrative a fairy-tale quality. We are introduced to the woodlands and surrounding park where the school is located: a place with high stone walls and metal grates in the forest floor, indicating that this is a maintained natural space with a built infrastructure, rather than wild nature. We enter dark tunnels that are empty and silent, and we see a door with the number three in a series of static shots. We hear scratchy diegetic music and a girl in white, shot from waist height, walks around the coffin that is now on the floor of a room. Five girls in white uniforms and ankle boots—a sixth, the tallest—unlock and open the coffin to reveal the sleeping form of Iris (Zoé Auclair) who slowly opens her eyes. She sits up and they ask her name, and she's introduced to the others by Bianca as they help Iris to dress.[1]

Hair ribbons are exchanged amongst the girls in a clear indication of hierarchy according to age and length of time at the school, and this is one of the film's many potent, silent gestures. Iris is shown the school, its grounds, its ways. Here, we can see that individuality is tightly controlled: hairstyles vary (though always ponytails or braids) and the color coding of the ribbons segregates the girls into distinct age groups, while all other clothing remains the same: a white blouse, skirt, and jacket along with white socks and brown walking boots. There are lots of opportunities for play, but only within the grounds, and while there is plenty of chatter and laughter, there is little in the way of substantial dialogue and answers to questions are often elliptical. There are rules for being a girl in *Innocence*: it is about learning boundaries and how to be "correct." We might also reflect on the phrase "tenue correcte" which references the idea of appropriate clothing or appropriate attire. In Sciamma's *Water Lilies* (which will be discussed in the next chapter), the synchronized swimming teams are inspected closely to ensure they have depilated their body hair prior to a competition, but this is also couched in terms of producing a "tenue correcte" in terms of a hairless armpit and ensuring no pubic hair is visible beyond the boundaries of the swimsuits. In *Innocence*, there is nothing so explicitly strict as this, but the threat of punishment for transgression is discussed by the girls since those who try to escape are never seen again. The girls arrive in silence into the world of the school wearing only their underwear, and they are never offered any fuller explanation for why things are the way they are—girls are expected to comply with the circumstances in which they find themselves. In *Innocence*, we see girls who do not even suspect there might be other ways of being, because they have been kept in such a carefully controlled environment. In this sense, the silence that surrounds them appears on first inspection as calming and pastoral, but in fact it proves to be a disciplining silence that keeps them in a state of forced innocence,

---

[1] We see this kind of sororal, feminine bonding in Peter Weir's *Picnic at Hanging Rock*, and to an extent in Sciamma's *Bande des Filles*. These kinds of spaces and moments can also be suffused with eroticism (as it is in Sciamma's *Water Lilies*) though that element is absent in *Innocence*.

recalling Paul Théberge's conceptualization of silence as a texture that can be perceived as tranquil or abnormal.

When Iris asks about her little brother, why there are no boys around Bianca simply replies "parce que [because]" and Iris never pursues this further, accepting this response. Iris is then distracted by the pleasures of being taught to swim in the lake (see Figure 5) by her housemates. Here, the girls watch and aid Iris, gently instructing her how to move her limbs. As can be seen in the image below, she is surrounded by tender, shared gazes, and supported by Bianca as she learns to let the water hold her body. The swimming here is playful and unsupervised by adults, making it markedly different from the sea bathing we see in *Evolution*. In *Evolution*, sea bathing is closely monitored by adult women, and the boys are admonished for swimming alone or out of sight, for fear the strong currents may carry them away. In *Innocence*, the choice of a lake versus the sea is significant in terms of the gendered worlds on offer in each film—girls are allowed to swim, but in a stiller and more closely boundaried body of water, while boys bathe in the openness of the sea, playfighting and exploring the ocean floor and the shoreline. Here too, the waters in which the children play reflect the qualities of their surroundings: silence as protective, and silence as dangerous.

When the girls enter their house for supper, Iris is introduced to Madeleine (Micheline Hadžhalilović), one of several silent, gray-haired women who act as servants in the school, alongside the two young teachers Edith (Hélène de Fougerolles) and Eva (Marion Cotillard). Edith and Eva are the only adult

Figure 5 Iris (Zoé Auclair, center) is taught to swim by her housemates in *Innocence*.

characters with any substantial speaking presence in *Innocence*, apart from the voice of an unseen adult man who throws Bianca a rose on her final night dancing in the school's secret theater. As Iris is put to bed, Bianca sets off on her evening errand, calmly refusing to stay with Iris or reveal her errand's purpose. In this sense, Bianca also sets up a strict boundary where she will not be cajoled by Iris into staying with her or revealing where she is going—Bianca's destination remains a secret from Iris, cloaked in silence. Bianca walks alone along a wooded path illuminated by electric lights, once more reinforcing the woodland setting as one that is tended and surveilled, rather than wild and untamed.

Innocence (like Sciamma's *Waterliles* and *Girlhood*) also captures the silent jealousies of girls' friendships, and how Bianca is sister, mother, and peer to Iris, who places all her need for protection and reassurance with Bianca. Bianca unquestioningly accepts this responsibility, and never grows impatient with Iris, demonstrating a perfectly serene and well-integrated care-giving instinct. This too is part of the silent, implicit education offered to girls in the world of *Innocence*—they are simply given responsibilities which they are expected to uphold. The film shows the helplessness of the youngest girls, and how the older ones "naturally" look after them; on the one hand, this is a moving expression of communal tenderness, and on the other it presents these relationships as a fait accompli, with no other option available. This kind of contented belonging is rare, but *Innocence* presents it as common, fostered by the closed environment of the school. Helplessness is part of the structure of femininity and girlhood on show here—it is a quality that is supposed to make other people want to care for you, to help you, to protect you. In the world of *Innocence*, helplessness does seem to result in being cared for and therefore this quality is reinforced as part of the girls' implicit education. As with many of the other qualities that are cultivated in the girls here, this one is silent, and never explicitly discussed.

The classroom of Mademoiselle Edith is where the girls learn about the natural world, which includes themselves and their bodies. This instruction is complimented by ballet class with Mademoiselle Eva, who tells her pupils they must work hard as she gives them a series of warm-up movements at the barre. Here, ballet offers rigor to the body—it is not dance as a personal expression, but as bodily discipline. This too feeds into conventional ideas about how the feminine body should look, that the "correct" body comes out of hard work, work that is surveilled and judged by others, and that never looks explicitly like a sport.

Out of doors, the girls play at dancing, and with hoops and ribbons as well as swings—a world where fine weather feels endless and the girls seem to enjoy lots of unstructured time. Iris continues to be curious about what Bianca does at night and tries to follow her, only to end up running through the dark woods to be found by her housemates. They then tell her the punishment for trying to leave the grounds is to stay at the school forever as a servant. While the school is a place that seems pleasant on the surface, the idea of remaining there forever is clearly a distressing threat. This interdiction once more aligns *Innocence* with conventions of fairy tale, as Summer Brennan remarks: "In fairy tales women and girls are often asked to pay a price of pain, or silence, or both" (96). In *Innocence*, the price of transgression is both pain and silence, if not death, since girls who disappear are never spoken of again.

In spite of these interdictions, there are spaces where the girls try to work out how to get to the outside—the grates in the ground, a section of wall with drawings and notes pushed into the spaces in the stone—the examination of and discussion of these spaces indicate the presence of a rebellious undercurrent within the school. This sense of what lies beneath the seemingly idyllic surface of this community is furthered when we see Iris and Selma (Alisson Lalieux) play together, but Selma becomes violent, beating Iris with a long bullrush across her legs, fascinated by Iris's distress. This move from gentleness to violence indicates that efforts to suppress certain impulses within the pupils have not succeeded. When Iris asks to get into bed with Bianca, she's told this is a forbidden act ("c'est interdit"), showing Bianca to be someone who is clearly intent on functioning within a system she may not even perceive as being capable of oppression.

In dance class the following day, Eva tells Iris "obedience is the only path to happiness," something that Bianca has already unwittingly internalized. This statement suggests that it is useless to fight these largely silent structures, especially when you don't even know what they are or where they begin and end. This too is at the core of the silence of *Innocence*, the silence of the baked-in ignorance imposed under the guise of maintaining an ideal about girls who know nothing of the outside world. Brennan also remarks on this idea: "We train girls from a young age to look forward to that someday when their prince will come, the tiny shoe will fit, and their happily ever after will begin" (2019: 89). The only sign we have that Bianca may eventually reject the path that has been chosen for her is when we discover she keeps a hidden memento box, though she disposes of the items it contains the following day. The items in this box promise pleasure and sexuality, but gaining access to this promise may also be conditional on Bianca's continued compliance.

A significant moment in the film occurs when Laura (Olga Peytavi-Müller) tries to escape in a boat across the lake. Her row boat fills with water and she drowns, never to be seen again. As a storm rages, Alice tells the others that the stories of punishment are just there to scare them—Alice has become suspicious of the structures that surround them. Bianca finds Iris hiding in the toilets, frightened by the storm and her knowledge that Laura took the boat and she is afraid both she and Laura will be punished. Laura is given an elaborate funeral, her tiny coffin burnt on a pyre as her classmates look on, and in this sense her death is highly visible, but conducted largely in silence, as if there is no need to discuss the matter further. Here, the lack of discussion around Laura's death, the fact that it occurred as she was attempting to escape, maintains a sense of taboo or forbidden topics that cannot be openly discussed.

At New Year, we see a dinner taking place at the school in a large room with all the houses assembled along with both teachers. The presence of the girls during this holiday suggests they may not have parents, and that the school is their only home. Alice hopes to be chosen by the headmistress to leave the school (to what end remains mysterious). Alice and other blue ribbon girls perform for the headmistress, and each girl is inspected in return for the quality of her profile, the length of her neck, her ability to stay in demi-pointe. Their teeth and hands are exposed for examination, but Alice is not chosen and faints from the pressure. There is something both familiar and sinister about this sequence—the tender voices of the older women as they carry out their observations, and the wordless acquiescence of the girls cultivate an atmosphere of probing examination, where the girls are treated like pampered pets, but ones that are being reared for a particular purpose. This atmosphere is taken to an even further horrifying expression in Hadžhalilović's *Evolution*.

In spring, we see the eldest girls being instructed about insect metamorphosis, as Mademoiselle Edith explains menarche and puberty to the girls with purple ribbons. Soon after this, we see Bianca rising from her bath, and she briefly glimpses her naked body in the bathroom mirror. It is clear that Bianca can see her body is changing but it is unclear how she feels about it, not unlike the wordless anxiety experienced by Laure/Mikaël in *Tomboy*. This is another instance of that curious, ambiguous child gaze that looks out at the world and wonders about how to make sense of it. As Lebeau remarks:

> Innocence, sexuality—are themselves so deeply implicated in the work of sustaining the ideal of childhood as symbol of the good, the natural, the pure ... the compulsion to render the child sexless, to present her nudity as symbol of her primordial innocence ... tends to have the effect of sexualizing the child through the look that comes *at* her or him.
>
> (2008: 98)

Here, the look that comes at Bianca is her own gaze reflected in the bathroom mirror. It is distanced, fleeting, as if she is not even sure she wishes to confront the reality of her changing body. This moment in particular reinforces some of the texture of *Innocence*'s unsettling silence, drawing attention to the fact that just as Bianca is not certain of her own body, the audience are not quite sure how to look at this film. *Innocence* portrays a particularly rigid version of girlhood, but it is one that nonetheless calls into question the value of delicacy and compliance as qualities that might be desired in young girls.

Raised in this highly structured and closed environment, Bianca takes the next eldest girl (soon to be her successor) through a secret door in the grandfather clock, into the school's underground theater where white-clad ballerinas with gauze butterfly wings perform before a shadowy audience. As Eva gives Bianca menstrual products, she tells her it's her last night at the theater, and that the eldest girls will soon leave the school. As Bianca dances on stage in her white costume an adult male voice calls out to her "bravo, t'es la plus belle" and throws a rose onto the stage which Bianca tucks under the strap of her leotard. This rose reappears later when we see Bianca examining her secret box of mementos. This box contains an engraving of a male nude from antiquity, a pink glove left behind in the theater, and the rose thrown on the stage. Bianca puts on the glove and caresses her legs—a close-up shot of this gesture shows only her torso and hand, but the gesture is both exploratory and sensuous, suggesting she is curious about her own desires and her own body.

The next day Bianca throws the glove and the rose into the lake—discarding the things she desires but does not know how to articulate or ask for. This gesture signals her ambivalence: that she is curious, but does not wish to leave behind the world of childhood just yet. Lebeau remarks on the reception of *Innocence* noting that "[film critic Philip] French looks for the paedophilic gaze as cause, and presumably, as construct of Hadžhalilović's film" (2008: 120) and while there are sinister instances of the surveillance of girls' bodies, the moment where we see Bianca deploying these objects she has chosen to keep suggests something closer to experimentation and the discovery of sexuality. In this sense, the silence of *Innocence* creates a container where these two ways of looking (at the self) and being looked at (by others) can coexist. This brief interlude suggests that Bianca may be on her way to a greater sense of self-actualization, and that this gesture has more in common with the solo fantasies played out by D in Joanna Hogg's *Exhibition*. While I don't wish to suggest that Bianca demonstrates an adult sexuality here, there is certainly a suggestion of beginning to explore new and complex feelings and the sensations that can accompany the onset of puberty, and these feelings and sensations present themselves even in highly structured and repressive environments.

So often for girls, the discovery and exploration of sexuality are a double-edged sword and part of the power of the silences in *Innocence* makes a space for considering this idea. We see this when Bianca and another girl descend into the tunnels from the theater, where they meet one of the gray-haired women who shows them a box of money, telling them "who else would pay for you" and that this is how the school covers its costs. This woman also comments on Bianca's legs, "you'll know how to best make use of your legs when you're outside"—implying that this will be something Bianca can show off for money. At this comment, Bianca declares "je veux pas aller dehors/I don't want to go outside"—another instance of refusal, of not wishing to exit the world of childhood unless it is on her own terms. This older woman's stare suggests an outside world that places girls into a marketplace defined by sexual value, and that this is something Bianca will participate in (perhaps whether she wants to or not).

As Bianca and the oldest girls prepare to depart, she embraces each of her housemates and Madeleine before running off. The silent, gray-haired women unlock a series of underground passages and in a parallel sequence another small coffin is carried in and a new girl enters the school. Edith gathers up the now discarded purple hair ribbons and leads the eldest girls through the underground tunnels to a train carriage. On the short train journey, Eva lights a cigarette, and Bianca asks what will happen to them and Eva replies "you will forget us very quickly."

The girls are wordlessly handed over to two other women, who silently escort them away from Eva and Edith. The group exit a grand train station into a modern courtyard with fountains surrounded by glass-fronted buildings. The girls remove their shoes and begin to wade into the fountain, totally unselfconscious. Boys play near them and as Bianca goes into the fountain, she glimpses a boy through the jets of water, and they begin to splash one another, smiling hesitantly. This boy captures Bianca's emerging curiosity, and as they share a silent gaze there is a sense of not fully appraising, a gaze unused to looking at a boy in the flesh. As can be seen in Figure 6, Bianca smiles, but something is held back—her expression is neither the unselfconscious excitement of a child, but nor is it coy or seductive. An innocent but curious

Figure 6 Bianca (Bérangère Haubruge) in the fountain at the end of *Innocence*.

gaze, underscored by her experiment with the engraving, glove, and rose—here, silence becomes the ground for a growing awareness of the "new cycle." Yet, this jet of water is still between Bianca and the boy—the flood of culture, but also the flood of feeling that comes with adolescence.

There is a clear sense in all three of the films under discussion in this chapter that children have their own gaze that they share with one another and that they are often acutely curious about and attuned to the feelings of others. Iris is curious about Bianca. Nicolas is curious about but also wary of all the adult women who are supposed to look after him. Mroz also remarks on the qualities of the child gaze in Hadžhalilović's work:

> During a walk in the park, for example, Bianca and Iris come upon a deer grazing on a path. They watch it for a moment before it skips away into the undergrowth. The film here draws out a moment that resonates with an uncertain importance; it pulsates with a significance, suggested partly by the film's focus on Iris's intense gaze, which nevertheless remains ambiguous.
>
> (Mroz: 296)

The ambiguity of the child gaze here is part of what makes it challenging to write about, particularly when coupled with silence. The child's limited vocabulary, or their unwillingness to voice certain thoughts, can create a barrier and yet the existence of these films suggests a deep desire to acknowledge the subjectivity of children and an attempt to represent how they see the world and each other. These films are entirely distinct from the idea of films "for children" designed to entertain younger audiences. In the work of Sciamma and Hadžhalilović the child characters and how they perceive the world are complex and ambiguous. Rather than the woman as the unknowable subject, it may in fact be the child who keeps their secrets.

Vicky LeBeau observes:

> The small child tends to be discovered at the limits of what words can be called upon to tell, or to mean—a limit that then generates the questions of how to convey the child's experience in language, of what in that experience, of what *in the image*, falls outside of, and so resists the world of words.
>
> (2008: 10)

In all three of these films, silence and the framing and foregrounding of a child gaze work to offer up opportunities for considering the child's experience, and particularly those experiences that cannot yet be framed adequately in language by the child protagonists. Katharina Lindner's remarks on the body of the female dancer are pertinent here in considering the ways in which the girls of *Innocence* are surveilled and how those child characters perceive that surveillance: "The female dancer's existence is ambiguously alienated and disembodied in the sense that the body is subjectively perceived, while at the same time it is vigorously observed, scrutinised and compared to a (virtually unattainable) ideal" (2011: 3). In *Innocence*, girls are shown to the mysterious headmistress (played by Corinne Marchand, who some may recognize from her early role as Cléo in Agnès Varda's *Cléo de 5 à 7*) while their physical appearance is evaluated against an invisible standard. The exact purpose of this evaluation remains opaque, but the largely silent docility which the girls demonstrate and the pleasure they seem to take in being observed and judged as "correct" resonates with some of what Lindner asserts about the bodies of adult women dancers on film.

As can be seen in Figure 7, this demonstration in *Innocence* forms an important connection to the explicitly medical gaze that the boys are subjected to in *Evolution*. The boys do not take comfort in this type of gaze, perhaps because the medical setting is more tinged with fear and opacity than the

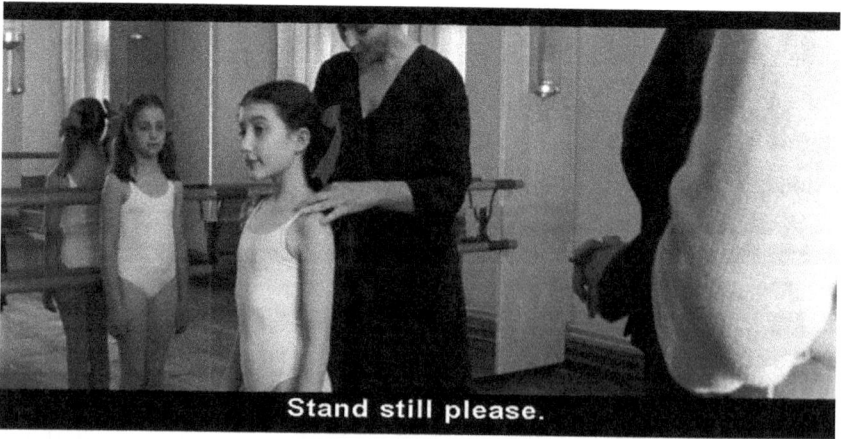

Figure 7 A pupil is shown to the headmistress in *Innocence*.

mirrored dance studio. The girls of *Innocence* have been raised to this kind of docility, and do not even seem to perceive this as sinister surveillance because they have become used to being watched, and in Figure 7 both pupils appear placid and calm. By contrast, the boys of *Evolution* seem to sense immediately that something is not right, and that they have reason to feel uncomfortable and suspicious. It is telling that Alice, the girl who is most vocal about her desire to be chosen by the headmistress, becomes unwell when things don't go her way. She faints, and then lies listless in bed, clearly depressed as Eva and her housemates tend to her. Alice gazes out at the frozen grounds before deciding to climb the wall, and sets off alone into the woods beyond the school. The other girls are told that Alice won't be mentioned again, silencing discussion of her departure. Having failed to be validated by the existing system, Alice finds she can no longer tolerate the regimented atmosphere of the boarding school. Her disappearance suggests that it is indeed possible to exit its confining structures, and her fate remains unknown, though different from Laura's attempt which results in death. Even though Alice is never spoken of again, her escape into the forest might be aligned with the way that adolescent characters escape their own confines. In the next chapter, I discuss how in Sciamma's *Girlhood*, Vic exits the frame at the end of the narrative, as if escaping into another story. Laura's and Alice's exits may be read as a precursor to this more radical exit, signaling another possibility entirely different from Bianca's more traditional trajectory of good, obedient adherence to the rules, before being seamlessly inserted into a heterosexual awakening in the fountain at the film's conclusion.

Evolution

Evolution also begins with the sound of water. In a series of spectacular shots of the dynamic ocean floor, the sea is established as a force but also a place, though we are not yet sure whether this is a place of refuge or terror. This is also a film filled with the sound of wind, moist sea creature bodies, and the sound of Nicolas (Max Brebant) drawing as he makes decisive marks on paper. Like the girls of *Innocence*, the boys of *Evolution* are also in a confined space, but rather than school grounds, this is the island where they live. Rather than being surrounded by woods and walls, they are surrounded by ocean in a barren, rocky landscape. In addition to this, they are subject to the confines of the hospital where mysterious experiments are carried out on their bodies.

As can be seen in Figure 8, the boys are surrounded by women who act as caregivers, and while on cursory inspection these relationships look normative, they are in fact a demonstration of what Maggie Nelson describes as "caretaking as detachable from—and attachable to—any gender, any sentient being" (2015: 90). Many of the gestures offered by these women are intended to be tender or protective, though we perceive through Nicolas's largely silent gaze that this tenderness shifts into something else. This shift and the eerie silence that pervades *Evolution* in terms of both caregiving figures and their charges bear certain similarities with the silences on display in *A Question of Silence* and *The Silences of the Palace*. In *Evolution*, silence is a container for medicalized violence, and the forbidden questions around the boys' origins. There is also a strong similarity with the tense silences of Claire Denis's controversial horror film *Trouble Every Day* (2001). In a key early moment, two young men break into the house where Coré (Beatrice Dalle) has been barricaded. Drawn silently toward her animal-like presence, one young man seems in the grip of an erotic trance when he rips off the wooden slats that bar the door to Coré's room as she stares hungrily at him. The sequence has no dialogue, but is filled with fascination, lust, and destruction as the atmosphere shifts between fear, desire, and dismemberment as Coré silently seduces and

Figure 8 Women supervise boys bathing in *Evolution*.

then noisily devours the intruder. This shift from the frisson of want and curiosity to something more predatory and horrifying also characterizes some of the silences we encounter in *Evolution*.

In *Evolution*, the silence of the child gaze creates a space for uncovering unsettling possibilities—in the world of the film, maternity is something that can be forced onto the child body. In many ways, this is a film that depicts the horror of forced birth, of implantation and pregnancy on unwitting subjects, and this aspect makes the incomprehension of the child gaze even more painful. While all the child protagonists in these films are attuned to feeling, the boys of *Evolution* do not fully understand the alien physicality of the caregiving figures that surround them, nor do they know they themselves are being impregnated until Nicolas sees it for himself, on his own body.

Silent Rituals

Stella (Roxane Duran) is a nurse who first appears stitching Nicolas's hand after he cuts it on the rocks. She tells him he's a good boy but he looks at her warily. That night, a procession of women convenes on the beach with lanterns. One of them holds a child-sized body wrapped in a sheet, and they gather around it, saying nothing. This is one of the first instances of potent, silent, gesture in the film, and the first of two ritual gatherings. There are two types of women in *Evolution*—the women who act as caregivers who gather on the beach, and those who work in the hospital carrying out tests and physical experiments. None of these adult figures ever seem to confer with one another, nor do they articulate why they are carrying out these tasks. The mysterious motives of these women are reinforced by dream-like sequences, such as the one where we see them eating raw sea urchin in the tidal pools. When Nicolas and Victor (Mathieu Goldfarb) go to the beach "to see what they do at night," they are confronted with the cephalopodesque nature of these beings: a writhing, moaning, slimy group on the sand. Shot in deep shadow, and filled with indeterminate sounds of slithering, it is unclear what they are doing—eating? Communing with unseen powers? Alongside these beach gatherings we also see hospital workers silently and unflinchingly watching videos of a live caesarean birth. These silent rituals, only one of which is witnessed by Nicolas and the other boys, suggest that adult life remains opaque in its meaning, reinforcing incomprehension as an aspect of what the child sees while maintaining their curiosity and suspicion.

When Nicolas is taken to the hospital, we hear the sound of instruments as he has his blood pressure checked: the Velcro sleeve, the hand pump, the snap of latex gloves, the brush of fabric gowns, and metal against metal. Stella takes a blood sample and Nicolas asks if he's going to die, to which Stella and the doctor say nothing. When Stella takes his sketchbook he snatches it back, and she tells him she wants to see his drawings and that she can keep a secret, setting up an atmosphere of weird intimacy. Nicolas is then prepped for surgery: he is given anaesthetic, and his abdomen is swabbed with an iodine-like liquid. As can be seen in Figure 9, a large syringe is inserted just below his navel while he is still conscious, but sedated. The framing here reinforces Nicolas's powerless position; drugged and strapped to the metal gurney, he can only look at what is being done to his body.

He reawakens in a hospital ward with other boys and one of them comes into the ward to show off his bandaged abdomen: "look what they did to me." Shortly after this, Nicolas glimpses the octopus-like suckers on his mother's back as she showers, confirming his suspicion that she is a being who is even

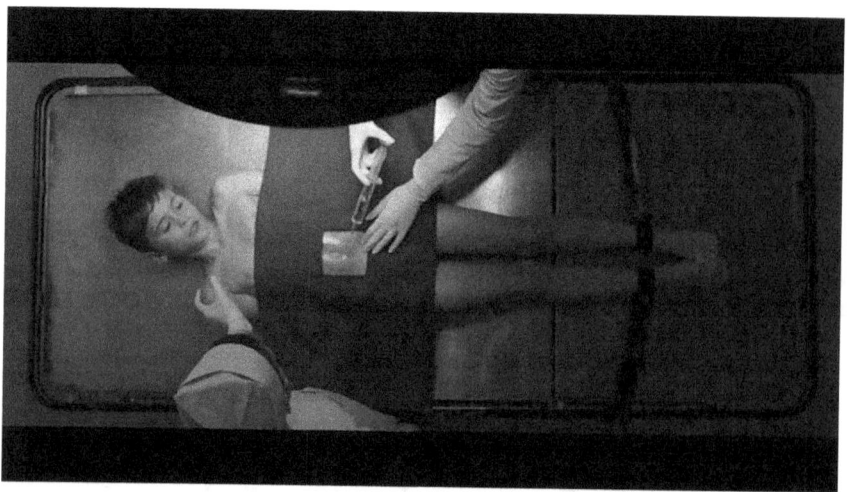

Figure 9 Nicolas injected in *Evolution*.

more different from him than he thought, and that she may not even be his mother. When Nicolas gets an ultrasound, his stomach appears bruised and we hear a sound like a foetal heartbeat. He returns to the ward where he's helped to undress for bed, and is met with silence when he asks, "How long do we have to stay here?" The silent horror of *Evolution* begins to emerge even more strongly at this stage, as Stella places three bloodied, embryo-like lumps into a specimen jar, while behind her Victor lies dead on the operating table. As he recovers in hospital, Nicolas's mother (Julie-Marie Parmentier) visits and offers him the same slimy green noodles we see him eating at the beginning of the film. He spits them out, and begins to rebel, shouting "you're not my mother!" In response to this rebellion, he is once more strapped to a gurney and given injections, effectively restraining, sedating, and silencing him. After Nicolas's outburst in the ward, the other boys begin to question things, with one telling the others, "My mother is not my mother."

When we see a more detailed ultrasound image of Nicolas's abdomen, we hear an underwater sound not unlike the soundscape that opens the film. Stella shows him "a secret"—a file of photographs of children from the hospital, suggesting records of a long-term experiment or study, once more hinting silently at the experiments and bodily transgressions that are taking place, and confirming the boys' suspicions. We realize that a silent affinity has been growing between Stella and Nicolas when we see them sitting together by the water. She undresses and he gently touches the suckers on her back. Swimming underwater together he struggles to hold his breath and she has to revive him back on land, where she cries with relief when he starts breathing. Nicolas is prepped for surgery a second time, and when he awakens he finds himself restrained in a large, dirty water tank. He looks down to see two suckling infant figures attached to his abdomen.

These infant beings seem to be semi-amphibious, able to live in and out of water and Nicolas is understandably horrified by this discovery which confirms what he has long suspected. When we next see Stella and Nicolas underwater, they are joined at the mouth. Stella swims while Nicolas clings to her, like a symbiote. This explicit pairing of pre-adolescent boy and adult woman is discomfiting, perhaps even more than some of the uneasy moments in *Innocence*. The film ends with Stella and Nicolas in a small row boat, where

Stella abandons Nicolas to drift alone until he reaches a distant refinery. Nicolas has left the insulated world of the island, but he is alone and unprotected and we have no idea what lies ahead for him. Where the girls of *Innocence* are at least left in the care of other teachers, there is no safety net for the boys of *Evolution*, who are used, disposed of, or cast out. Where silence might still be said to offer some measure of protection to the girls of *Innocence*, there is nothing for Nicolas at the end of *Evolution* except to forge his way alone. In *Evolution*, there is little sense of a shared child gaze, since Nicolas's most sustained relationships are with adult women. There is no sense of belonging or safety for these boys, which is radically different from the sense of what is to come for the girls of *Innocence*, or the possibilities of *Tomboy*.

Tomboy

Not being boy enough meant being hurt, damaged by other boys who were boy enough ... Boying here is about inclusion, friendships, participation approval. Boying here is about the cost of not being included. To want happiness for a child can be to want to straighten the child out. Maybe sometimes too, a boy might "self-boy" realising that he might have more friends, enjoy himself more, if he does the same things other boys do.

(Ahmed: 51)

In Sciamma's *Tomboy* we are in radically different territory from Hadžhalilović. Rather than the cold, structured worlds of *Innocence* and *Evolution*, we are introduced to a child protagonist without a name, without anything that openly signifies binary gender, but contained in a warm and tender family structure. Lindner comments on this introductory sequence in her book *Film Bodies*, noting, "It is rather presumptuous to use a gendered pronoun, and to refer to Laure as 'she' at this point as conventional markers of gender and sexual difference are notably absent" (2018: 206). The child (Zoé Héran) travels with their father (Mathieu Demy) and arrives at a new home, where their mother (Sophie Cattani) shows them to a blue-painted bedroom "like you wanted." On meeting their neighbor Lisa (Jeanne Disson), our protagonist gives their name as Mikäel.

Sciamma, like Hadžhalilović, excels at centering the gaze of her young protagonists. So much of *Tomboy* is a window into Laure/Mickäel's interactions with their sister Jeanne (Malonn Lévana), Lisa, and other playmates. Lindner observes that it is only after self-boying that Laure/Mickäel's gender, appearance, and actions can be read in certain ways.

> It is when she goes along with the (mis)recognition and begins to pass as a boy that her (entirely unaltered) appearance and behaviours take on transgendered implications. This is crucial as the variances in what her (tom)boyish demeanour *means* and how it is *read*—by Laure's family ("she is a girl"); by other children in the film ("this is a boy"); and, in rather different, shifting manner, by the spectator ("is this a (tom)boyish girl who passes as a boy?"; "is this 'really' a boy?"; "is this a trans boy?")—is entirely dependent on the knowledge and experience that we bring to the encounter, exposing the conditionality of visibility, legibility and appearance.
>
> (2018: 202)

In Hadžhalilović's work there is no question about how gender is read or what behaviors are expected, and the worlds in which her protagonists exist are cold and rigid. In *Tomboy*, the possibility of embodying different gender expressions and behaviors is presented as part of the curious child gaze, and Laure/Mikäel's narrative is facilitated by the variance on offer in the child gaze, in terms of both the self-gaze and the shared gaze of other children. Rather than being a place for silent dread and suspicion, in *Tomboy* the child gaze is a place of warm possibility.

Sciamma draws out any clear naming of her protagonist and it is only when the siblings are sharing a bath that they are finally named. Jeanne is the youngest, and then their mother calls for "Laure" and Mickäel rises from the bath, revealing a body with a flat pubic mound. The film doesn't use explicitly gendered feminine language for a good ten minutes, and in French this is no small feat. This bathing scene contains something like physical discomfort—not self-hatred, not quite shame, but perhaps some anxiety triggered by the name "Laure" and the scenario of confronting a part of the body that is used to designate sex at birth. In this sense, there is something of Bianca's discomfort with her mirror reflection in *Innocence*, though nothing like the fear and horror encountered by Nicolas in *Evolution* when he confronts his body as a vessel for forced pregnancy. Lindner remarks that in *Tomboy* the home is a space "where Laure's gender-nonconformity, including her androgynous/boyish appearance, behaviours and tastes are not only accepted but supported" (201). When Laure/Mickäel is given their own housekey on a pink lanyard, they immediately swap this for a plain white shoelace, suggesting that they know the significance of these color-coded symbols just as the girls of *Innocence* understand the meaning of their hair ribbons. Here too, clothing and color are signs that help the child protagonist to inhabit the world, and this deliberate gesture by Laure/Mickäel to choose a color that does not explicitly gender them can be read as an instance of Ahmed's "self boying." This swapping of the housekey lanyard, alongside the blue bedroom, short hair, and choice of clothes (all choices clearly supported by their parents), ensures that our protagonist passes easily for a boy, and that those cultural markers so often associated with "girlness" or femininity particularly in childhood (florals, pink) are deliberately being eschewed by Laure/Mickäel. When Laure/Mickäel and Lisa watch their playmates at football, we see that some of the boys have removed their shirts. On this first occasion Laure/Mickäel hangs back, but later examines their flat torso in the bathroom mirror, an assessment of "boyness" prompting them to join the next game of football, remove their shirt, and spit on the ground after a display of sporting success. Here, Laure/Mickäel pushes further into the realm of "self-boying," observing the conventions of those they wish to befriend more deeply, which also includes capturing the shy, admiring gaze of Lisa.

When Lisa and Laure/Mickäel socialize away from the rest of the group, we see them dancing in her bedroom, and Laure/Mickäel even allows Lisa to put make-up on them, and Lisa comments "'t'es bien en fille" "you look good as a girl" and reveals that they'll go swimming with the rest of the group the next day. Walking back home, Laure/Mickäel has not removed the make-up, but has drawn up their hood. On entering the flat, their mother calls out and is pleased by the make-up, perhaps interpreting this as an end to "tomboyness" and they fall happily into their mother's embrace. Outside the home, Mickäel clearly doesn't want others, particularly other boys, to see the make-up. However, they allow Lisa to apply the make-up as part of their play, indicating a willingness to play with codes in order to be close to Lisa, to develop their shared mutual gaze.

Already there is a sense that Mickäel sees women and girls as potentially more tolerant of femme expressions, whereas men may be hostile to this. This largely silent navigation of gender is presented in a multi-faceted way in *Tomboy*, where it is Mickäel's mother who is most distressed by the discovery that Laure has presented as a boy to their playmates, and Mickäel's father is more comforting and conciliatory. Once this "deception" has been revealed, Laure/Mickäel is rejected by all their playmates, but it is the boys who are most aggressive, wanting to determine Laure/Mickäel's gender and attach it to biological features, even goading Lisa to assist them in inspecting Mickäel's genitalia.

Before this revelation, Laure/Mickäel enjoys the opportunity to swim with their peers, a pleasure that is present across all three films. In *Innocence* and *Evolution*, swimming alone and with peers is a primary activity for the child protagonists as they interact with their friends and sometimes establish hierarchies. In *Innocence*, the girls of each house teach their newest classmate to swim in the lake, in *Evolution* boys swim alone or together and explore the shoreline, attacking and burying creatures they find there. In *Tomboy*, the swimming outing is particularly significant, since Laure/Mickäel must navigate this carefully. First, we see them cutting their one-piece swimsuit into trunks, and once more examining their silhouette in the mirror, knowing something is missing.

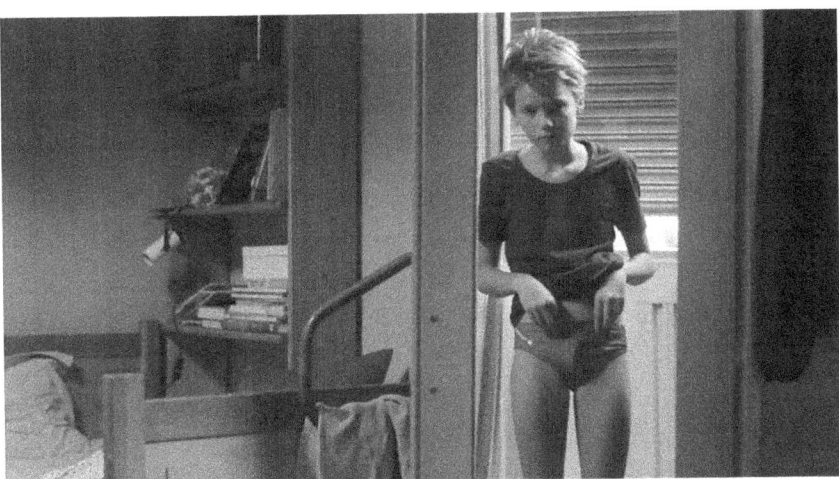

Figure 10 Laure/Mickäel (Zoé Héran) checks their swimsuit silhouette in *Tomboy*.

Mickäel makes a penis out of playdoh, and with this down the front of their trunks, the desired result is achieved, as can be seen in Figure 10, where they inspect their silhouette. We see the whole group swimming in a lake, with Laure/Mickäel wrestling with another boy on a plastic dock. Later, they even share a kiss with Lisa. After this success, Mickäel stores the ball of playdoh in a box containing their fallen milk teeth—a sign that this too is a body part that is precious, though perhaps not "discarded" so much as "tried on" and to be revisited. There is a parallel here with Bianca's memento box and Nicolas's sketchbook—these items are all repositories for the images and symbols that are important to the child protagonists of these films and their emergent personhood. These images and objects are rarely discussed with other children or adults, and it is significant that while adults ask to see Nicolas's drawings, he remains protective of these images. In contrast, Bianca and Laure/Mickäel keep their treasured objects entirely secret, never sharing or revealing them to anyone.

When Lisa next comes to fetch Laure/Mickäel to play, it is Jeanne who answers and when asked about the whereabouts of Mickäel she does nothing to dispel this perception, but asks her sibling on their return why they are "pretending to be a boy." Laure/Mickäel bargains with Jeanne, promising to bring her along to the group if she says nothing. Jeanne at six years old takes seamlessly to this idea of her sibling as a brother rather than a sister, even building her sibling's legend, telling her friend Cheyenne about her big brother's bravery in confronting her bullies. Jeanne is also enlisted to help Laure/Mickäel keep their hair short, and at dinner, after being made to promise not to give anything away, Jeanne tells her parents of her new friend Mickäel, and she and her sibling smile at one another across the table, a clear instance of a complicit child gaze. With this shared secret between them, the siblings are united.

When Laure/Mickäel fights a boy in Jeanne's defence, everything begins to unravel. When the boy and his mother come to Laure/Mickäel's home and at first their mother is confused at mentions of "your son" until Laure/Mickäel appears and admits to the fight. Their mother apologizes and says she will do the right thing and punish her child. She initially seems more upset about what she sees as the deception, and that Jeanne has been involved in what she sees as a lie. Perhaps rather unusually, it is their father who consoles Laure/Mickäel, and says it will all work out.

Laure/Mickäel's mother makes them put on a dress (a simple blue tunic but a dress nonetheless) to apologize and explain to all their playmates. When they go to Lisa's apartment, she is wordlessly upset, and Laure/Mickäel runs off into the woods. Their mother tells them she has to do this, that *she* doesn't mind about how they dress, or if they are "playing the boy" but school is starting—and this more formal structure is likely to bind the child into a more rigid binary, as we see with the girls of *Innocence*. In the woods, Laure/Mickäel leaves the dress hanging from a fallen tree, returning wearing shorts and a singlet, once more signaling their awareness and rejection of symbols they regard as too feminine for their gender expression. When the play group spot Laure/Mickäel, after having heard the news "Mickäel is a girl" they chase and corner them, wanting to "check" if Mickäel is a girl. As can be seen in Figure 11, it's unclear exactly what happens here, if Lise does indeed pull down Mickäel's shorts and reveal their genitals to the group. Later, we see them alone in the woods, head between their knees, clearly distressed by what has taken place. Linder's assessment of this moment coincides with my own reading: "Only their upper bodies are in the frame when Laure and Lisa

Figure 11 Lisa (Jeanne Disson) is goaded by her friends to look inside Laure/Mickäel's shorts in *Tomboy*.

stand facing each other. They continue to look at each other as Lisa seems to unzip or pull down Laure's shorts and then briefly glance downwards at Laure's crotch. We are unable to see exactly what Lisa does, and what exactly she sees" (221).

Some weeks later, the new baby has been born to Laure/Mickäel's mother, and school is about to start. Lise appears in the green below their balcony, prompting Laure/Mickäel to descend, and when Lisa asks "what's your name," they reply "Je m'apelle Laure." Lindner notes that the ending "is one of mutual acknowledgement that queers both characters" (222) and I admire Lindner's willingness to articulate the questions that arise from *Tomboy*'s ending:

> Does Laure go along with the initial (mis)recognition because she is attracted to Lisa? Can the gender disguise therefore be read as Laure's attempt to act on her (forbidden) desire for Lisa? Is Laure therefore a 'lesbian'? Or is she really just a (tom)boyish girl, so used to being misrecognised as a boy, that it is just easier, and perhaps more fun, to play along with it? Or does Laure genuinely feel like a boy, and want to be a boy? And are gender nonconformity and passing therefore manifestations of a trans identity?
>
> (Lindner 204)

It is all of these gently unresolved queries that "invite[s] a spectatorial attitude of openness and vulnerability that enables the film to make contact" (Lindner 207). I would also argue that this open attitude is facilitated by the film's quietude and silence, its willingness to not give things a name. This container of silence is part of what allows the film to construct its child gaze; it is what allows us to engage with this story without our own look taking anything from the subjectivity or autonomy of the film's predominantly young subjects. Lindner observes, "We no longer look at Laure looking at herself in the mirror, but we look in the mirror with her" (214). This idea of "looking with" is vital to the construction of the agency Sciamma grants to her protagonist in *Tomboy* and *Girlhood*. For Lindner, this agency is continuously affirmed through touch: "Laure takes off her shirt, again touching her stomach, a specifically tactile affirmation of the self, and then looks around to assess whether her exposed upper body has affected a change in her 'appearance'" (217). Looking and touching as a component of the child gaze also appear in *Innocence* when Bianca briefly glimpses her changing body in the mirror, and when she strokes her legs as she examines her mementos. But for Bianca, these are distant actions, as if she is not even sure that her body belongs to her. For Nicolas, he and the other boys examine their bodies only after they have been cut open, and his dreams of being touched by a slimy, snail-like appendage suggest a fear of certain kinds of touch. Where Hadžhalilović's children stare and touch their bodies with suspicion or distress, Sciamma's children are largely portrayed as having agency over how their bodies are presented. The exception to this is when Laure/Mickäel is forced to put on a dress, and when their playmates become aggressive. But even after these distressing events, Laure is still permitted a shy and tender reconciliation with Lisa at the film's conclusion.

In Hadžhalilović's work, girls are kept, while boys are abandoned. In *Tomboy*, the child is independent, but also lovingly parented. Girl as a "restricted category" is explored and elaborated in the next chapter, which deals much more explicitly with adolescence, and particularly sexual awakening. *Evolution*'s conclusion is very much about how we are alone, cast out to make our own way. In *Innocence* the adolescent girl is ceremoniously led into the outer world beyond the walls of the school, and through the fountain she sees a boy, and with him the promise of connection and belonging, though she does not know that with this comes the imposition of a cultural narrative that centers on the endless quest for physical perfection, and on a form of compulsory heterosexuality. There is promise here, but that promise is that the body is perilous. This is true for the girls in *Innocence* and true for the young people in *Water Lilies* and in *Girlhood*. At the end of those films, Vic and Floriane are alone. Vic runs out of the frame (into another story?) while Floriane dances alone in a room filled with people who are potential friends, lovers, and rivals, envious of her gilded beauty and perfection, not knowing what to do with what is perceived as her sexuality, a sexuality that she does not yet fully understand how to inhabit. Laure/Mickäel is ejected and then reintegrated. In both *Innocence* and *Evolution*, children are cast out of environments meant to offer "corporeal education" and to nurture them.

But part of this is the realization that what they have previously experienced as care is in part designed to make them compliant. Both the boys of *Evolution* and the girls of *Innocence* fear what happens to friends who disappear never to return. This silence around failure to comply, and around experiments in bodily autonomy will be explored further in the next chapter that deals with the trials of coming of age as an adolescent.

2

Adolescence and Collaborative Queer Gazes in *Water Lilies/Naissance des pieuvres*, and *Girlhood/Bande des Filles*

Joanna Walsh, writing about experiments in online identities, notes how silence can be interpreted: "Silence is a sign of system failure. Silence is also a system" (2022: 110). For the child protagonists of Hadžhalilović's films, silence becomes a system of oppression that must be broken, whereas in Sciamma's work silence becomes a place of contemplation where burgeoning (often queer) desires can be mutually explored. The way in which silence is deployed in both *Water Lilies* and *Girlhood* suggests a use of the gaze as articulated by the artist Kate Durbin "the girl gaze is like a fuck you to the male gaze." These films comprise a possible "fuck you" to the confines of girlhood as a stage and to the limitations of gender, class, and race that these protagonists encounter. While there is a certain degree of overlap between the curious silence of the child gaze discussed in the previous chapter, the films under discussion here will formulate some of the differences between the child gaze and that of the adolescents and young people that we follow in two films by Céline Sciamma: *Water Lilies/Naissance des pieuvres* (2007) and *Girlhood/Bande des Filles* (2014). *Water Lilies* contains moments of contemplative silence and quietude, as it explores an entangled web of friendships between its teenage protagonists: Marie (Pauline Acquart), Anne (Louise Blachère), and Floriane (Adèle Haenel). Marie and Anne are long-standing friends, but Anne's awkwardness and anxiety about her developing body make Marie reject her in favor of the popular, blonde Floriane. Marie is besotted with Floriane who subsequently befriends her, and their friendship shifts through moments of sexual initiation and desire which have subsequently been read as examples of lesbian and queer representation

(Bradbury-Rance 2019; Lindner 2018). The film is characterized by extended sequences without dialogue, focusing instead on the way in which the girls observe one another and develop a shared, collaborative gaze (a motif for establishing desire that Sciamma returns to in *Portrait of a Lady on Fire*). Here, Sciamma recalibrates what might otherwise be considered a display of a post-feminist culture of surveillance and (silent) judgment, instead allowing for the display of Marie's curiosity, anxiety, and budding queer desire, making space for a queer girl gaze.

Girlhood also portrays teen protagonists: Marieme/Vic (Karidja Touré), Lady (Assa Sylla), Adiatou (Lindsay Karamoh), and Fily (Mariétou Touré). Like *Water Lilies*, the film has extended sequences without dialogue which instead focus on shared gazes, looks, and stares. However, *Girlhood* also displays a technique similar to one deployed in Ramsay's *Morvern Callar*, where moments of intensity are underscored with an extra-diegetic soundtrack,[1] such as when Marieme is standing in her family's kitchen doing the dishes, and finds a pocket knife in the sink. She carefully slips the weapon into her back pocket and the camera draws back to show her from behind, as the music builds to create a mood of anticipation. The next shot we see of Marieme shows her dressed in the style of the gang she has just joined: her hair is straightened, similar to Lady and Adiatou, and she wears a black leather motorcycle jacket. Marieme, having become too large for the claustrophobic domestic space of her home, and thwarted in her desire to go on to high school by a racist and classist school system, makes a decision in front of the sink. The knife is the object that allows her to cross the threshold from the domestic world of her childhood, into the teenage girlhood of the gang. The absence of dialogue that might discuss or articulate her decision in more traditional terms signals the potential power of the girl gaze as a space for developing power and self-actualization through shared gazes, looks, and stares, to convey meaning in both of these films. The development of the importance of mutuality and community as girls gaze at one another in ways that convey support and the sense of being held by your

---

[1] Paul Théberge discusses this particular form of silence in greater detail in his chapter "Almost Silent: The Interplay of Sound and Silence in Contemporary Cinema and Television" in *Lowering the Boom: Critical Studies in Film Sound*. Edited by Jay Beck and Tony Grajeda. University of Illinois Press, 2008.

friends, as well as gazing out of the frame toward other possibilities, will be explored in relation to how silence and the absence of dialogue work to focus attention on the importance of the gaze.

Naissance des pieuvres/Water Lilies

The sense of girlhood as a transitional phase is explored in detail in *Water Lilies*, primarily through the use of a girl gaze. The film encompasses two potential kinds of gazing: a surveilling gaze and a nurturing gaze. As Clara Bradbury-Rance notes in her discussion of *Water Lilies* as lesbian cinema, "speech is often entirely abandoned in favour of other sensory expressions; desires remain unspoken … the intensity of verbal silence is made apparent by the aural dominance of Para One's musical score and the background chatter of nameless girls" (2019: 83). The film's textures of silence in terms of silent gazing overlaid by music or indistinct chatter work toward establishing a particular technique of silence as a space for establishing the affective presence of girls on screen who move beyond conventional coming-of-age narratives. Katharina Linder asks, "How does what is 'visible' on screen (absence, gaps, ambiguity) relate to what we 'see' (lesbianism)?" (2018: 22). The same question might be applied to silence and what it allows us to see in Sciamma's work. The verbal language of queer liberation does not find a home in Sciamma's work, but her silences do make a radical space of acceptance for a variety of queer sexualities to emerge. In this sense, the absence of identity labels in both of these films (and elsewhere in Sciamma's output) permits a greater range of intimacy and tenderness to be seen, understood, and recognized.

Both *Water Lilies* and *Girlhood* also explore the snap of desire, when the world becomes refocused through the overwhelming swoon of a crush, particularly when that is a queer crush that cannot be openly discussed or acknowledged. In a similar vein, Neil McCormick (Joseph Gordon Levitt) in Gregg Araki's *Mysterious Skin* (2004) describes his first sexual feelings as being "like a present I had to open in front of a crowd," a feeling that often characterizes narratives involving queer youth. Neil's remark is emblematic of how in many queer coming-of-age narratives there is almost always this sense of never being entirely safe, of being unsure, of being misread, of being subject to judgment. *Water Lilies* (alongside Sciamma's *Tomboy* and *Girlhood/Bande des Filles*) all navigate these feelings and they do so largely through looks, stares, shared gazes, and other non-verbal gestures. Crucially, *Water Lilies* and *Girlhood* are films that also create spaces where it is possible to express one's desires without experiencing violence as a result of that expression. The spaces that Sciamma chooses for the settings of these films are ordinary and sometimes semi-public locations such as the swim center changing room in *Water Lilies*, the playground and woods in *Tomboy*, and the streets and bedrooms of outer Paris in *Bande des Filles*. These everyday spaces recognize the fact that queer individuals and queer love are everywhere.

> *Water Lilies* articulates these two aspects of the girl gaze (the surveyant and the nuturing) via the representation of its three protagonists: Marie, Anne, and Floriane.
>   Girls in the sense we now use the word—encompassing no specific age group, but rather an idea of mobility preceding the fixity of womanhood and implying an unfinished process of personal development—are produced at a nexus of late modern ways of being in and knowing the world.
>
> (Driscoll 2002: 47)

Through Driscoll's phrase "the fixity of womanhood" we can consider how this concept structures girlhood as transitional, an unfinished status that implies a fixity might one day be achieved. But this too is something of a myth, since we are never really done with the project of the self, though we may grow in confidence, and wisdom, and we may achieve bodily comfort and satisfaction, no one remains fixed. Sciamma's films and the transitions undertaken by her adolescent protagonists articulate an increasingly visible common experience with regard to the fluidity of gender and sexuality, but also acknowledging the pace of change throughout life. It is therefore fitting that the three main characters in *Water Lilies* all experience girlhood differently, in accordance with the way they experience looking and embodiment. We might consider Driscoll's claims about the idea of girls in relation to the image of the waterlily, with its extensive, underwater root network that is usually invisible to the casual observer. The film's English title evokes several images: the beautiful formations of synchronized swimming alongside the mysteries of girls' interactions, suggesting that these may normally run below the waterline of visibility, but that Sciamma is at pains to make legible and visible in her film. Questions about sexual awakening and the realization of desire, as well as how it might be complicated by feelings of friendship are further suggested by the film's original French title *Naissance des pieuvres* which translates as "Birth of the Octopi." The choice of this image in the title suggests a deliberate resonance with Violette Leduc's queer coming-of-age novel *Thérèse and Isabelle*,[2] which also deals with a romance that develops between two adolescent girls. In the novel, Leduc thrice invokes the image of an octopus (pieuvre) in relation to budding lesbian desire "there is an octopus in my belly" (19) "if the creeping octopus would leave me" (23) "the octopus in my guts was quivering" (56). This unusual imagery is deployed by Leduc as an experimental method for articulating a language of queer desire and how it feels in the body. The film's French title alongside the ways in which synchonized swimmers are filmed underwater to show their churning, twisting limbs, also clearly evokes this imagery and the environment of the swimming pool itself becomes a site of the desiring girl gaze. As can be seen in Figure 12, the octopus as metaphor for desire is suggested by Marie's intense interest in viewing the elegant, intertwining legs of the synchronized swimmers. This is in contrast to the way Hadžhalilović silently evokes the alien and the cephalopod in *Evolution* as a source of threat, and in *Innocence* where girlness and femininity are rigidly enforced, almost as if the structures of the school may help to stem the forces of culture that cannot be controlled once the girls leave the grounds. In *Water Lilies*, imagery that evokes the octopus and the waterlily, the tentacle and the stem, makes for a particularly fluid and undulating atmosphere, one that has many potential tendrils that can encompass the film's focus on desiring girl gazes.[3]

Floriane (Adèle Haenel) initially presents as beautiful and bored, the captain of a competitive synchronized swimming team, she is slender and tanned, with

---

[2] While Leduc's novel was initially censored and suppressed, it was finally published in an unexpurgated version in 1966.

[3] As Maggie Nelson notes in *The Argonauts*, "I am interested in the fact that the clitoris, disguised as a discrete button, sweeps over the entire area [the pubic mound and anal cavity] like a manta ray, impossible to tell where its eight thousand nerves begin and end" (2015: 106).

Figure 12 Marie's underwater view of the synchronized swimmers rehearsing in *Water Lilies*.

a careless sultriness that evokes the young Brigitte Bardot, an image that is easy to read as a signal of sexual maturity. But her allure, which fascinates Marie, as well as numerous young men, is not without its disadvantages. Not only does Floriane's appearance create jealousy and animosity amongst her team mates, it also means she has been subject to a number of unwanted advances. Anne, at fifteen, is already in possession of a body that presents as physically mature, conforming to conventional representations of the "womanly" with her full breasts and hips. Where Floriane appears confident, Anne is profoundly confused by her body, particularly when she compares herself to the other girls she swims with, who are not only far shorter, but far smaller. Sciamma shows Anne's embarrassment about her body, when we see her waiting until the changing room is empty to remove her swimsuit after practice.

Marie is the same age as both Anne and Floriane, but appears far younger. Disappointed by what she perceives as her weak, too thin body (she too waits for the changing room to empty before donning her swimsuit), she openly declares to Anne "je ne suis pas normale/I am not normal" as we see her attempting weight lifting exercises to become stronger. Marie idolizes Floriane, whom she both admires and desires. Driscoll notes:

As bodily change in puberty is often represented as sexual development, sexual organs remain definitive indices of adolescence. Puberty is held to produce a quantitative and qualitative change in sexual desire and genital form and is, in this sense, an unwilled and uncontrollable assertion of the sexual body—an anatomical destiny that paradoxically requires channelling into proper sexual practices hitherto substantially alien to the child.

(2002: 84)

Driscoll's description of the way that puberty is often perceived via physical development aligns closely with the ways in which the bodies of Floriane and Anne are misread. Anne misreads her own body's maturity as a sign that she is, as she describes it "en retard" or "late" when it comes to other emotional and physical experiences. Her body presents as physically mature; therefore she feels under pressure to "channel [herself] into proper sexual practices," even though she still openly desires the kind of play and objects more commonly associated with childhood. This is exemplified in a sequence where Anne and Marie go to McDonalds. Anne requests a Happy Meal and has to argue with the cashier who says she is too old to order this item. We subsequently see Anne happily playing with the Happy Meal toy, which she states is the main reason she likes the Happy Meal. The way in which *Water Lilies* displays the cultural dissonance of Anne's experiences perfectly encapsulates what is sometimes perceived as the tension of adolescence, when one is urged to leave behind the pleasures of childhood in favor of entering into the realm of adult sexuality.

In this sense, Bianca's narrative trajectory in *Innocence* can be seen to map onto Anne's, where Bianca's curious gaze at the boy in the fountain can be compared with Anne's desires which encompass both a pleasure in toys and the desire to be kissed. By refusing to leave behind either of these pleasures, to not choose one over the other, Anne becomes a potentially radical form of adolescent girl who demands to explore play and pleasure, in contrast to Bianca's silent acquiescence and docility. The way in which *Water Lilies* attends to the nuances of how each character navigates the fragile zone of girlhood addresses some of the gaps in terms of valuing girlhood as an experience worthy of depiction. Kate Zambreno articulates this frustration about the perceived worth of narratives that explore "messy" or even "toxic" girlhoods:

> It's infuriating to think how coming-of-age novels about the feminine experience are read and dismissed as chick lit or school girl books, or YA, etc., … As if the female coming-of-age experience is somehow more frivolous or less rending than the male one. And how these works are seldom read as existential novels about girls who want to realise themselves.
>
> (Zambreno 2012: 193)

Zambreno's anger at the dismissal of female coming-of-age narratives in print may be somewhat absolved by the way in which *Water Lilies* (and *Girlhood*, for that matter) are very much treated as stories about girls who want to realize themselves. Even the girls who offer up some measure of resistance in *Innocence* may be regarded as girls who want to be free to construct their own identities.

Part of this coming-of-age narrative in *Water Lilies* includes an exploration of the ways in which each girl experiences her own body, as well as how they are perceived by others. Floriane's experiences are distinctly more sinister than Marie's or Anne's, and as the most conventionally beautiful, Floriane's looks and demeanor are consistently read as a sign not just of sexual availability, but of promiscuity. She tells Marie that older men have kissed her, and that men at the pool have exposed themselves to her. She shrugs this off declaring "ç'est la vie/that's life." But Marie has not encountered this form of harassment, and the presence of these distinct experiences within the film acknowledges the different ways girls experience patriarchy and the male gaze, indicating that Floriane's experiences are not simply a part of life that must be accepted. Realizing this, Floriane declares "t'as beaucoup de chance/you're lucky," and Marie *is* lucky that she has not had these experiences. As a reparative gesture, the film adopts Marie's silent gazing at Floriane as a way of making the queer girl gaze visible, and as a way of introducing the possibility of a more tentative, consensual, and nuturing gaze that may be shared between Floriane and Marie. While some of this silence may be interpreted as an instance of silence as "system failure," a failure to come out and declare oneself, to ask for what you want, I would argue that Sciamma's films make use of silence as a system, a platform for making felt and visible those girl gazes that have long be relegated or elided. Just as we do hear Floriane describe her experiences of being seen in a certain way by men, we also witness Marie and Anne's painful longing to be visible, particularly to their respective crushes, Floriane and François (Warren Jacquin).

Toxic Looks

There are also several instances where Floriane is surveilled not just by men, but by other girls. As she eats a banana after practice, one of Floriane's team mates admonishes and shames her, telling her that boys stare when a girl eats a banana in public, also remarking that Floriane is rumoured to have "done it" with several young men.

Floriane's response to this is a sneering "j'adore ça/I love it" as she continues to eat her banana (as can be seen in Figure 13), playing right into her reputation as someone who is sexually experienced. This occurrence reinforces the animosity and jealousy that Floriane's physical appearance and behavior provoke, regardless of the space she occupies. Floriane is still subject to a punishing gaze, despite the fact that she is the most conventionally beautiful, recalling how in *Innocence* Bianca is told by the male voice in the audience "t'es

Figure 13 Floriane (Adèle Haenel) sneers at her team mate admonishing her for eating a banana in *Water Lilies*.

la plus belle/you are the most beautiful." Floriane's reaction to this punishing gaze is to embrace her sexualized reputation, since she receives attention predominantly from men, while her female team mates dislike her. While Floriane's response here can be viewed as strategic, there is also something potentially reparative in her claiming of this position, and her refusal to be shamed by another's puritanical view. Not until she is approached by Marie does Floriane experience a nurturing female friendship, and while this is tinged by Marie's burgeoning queer desire, Clara Bradbury-Rance notes "an erotics of friendship need not supersede nor dissolve an erotics of lesbianism" (2019: 80). Marie's desiring gaze certainly seems to act as the one that is the least harmful to Floriane throughout the narrative, particularly because it also encompasses an erotics of care.

Driscoll asserts that "the proper accomplishment of puberty in adult sexuality demands distinctly gendered performances of heterosexuality and identity" (2002: 84) and we might consider this in light of the friendship between Marie and Floriane. Alongside their burgeoning friendship, Floriane accomplishes a "distinctly gendered performance" but Marie's queer desires also become visible through the conduit of their friendship. In turn, Floriane experiences the shared space of female companionship, something she lacks despite her role as swim team captain. Floriane's previously "excessive" beauty and perceived sexual promiscuity are modulated by Marie's presence as friend and adoring bearer of a queer crush. In this instance, the queer girl gaze acts as a space of protection and safety. In *Water Lilies*, the way desire is combined with friendship offers Floriane a temporary place of refuge from the misreading look of patriarchal culture, while simultaneously according visibility and importance to the on-screen presence of Marie's desiring queer girl gaze.

Marie's desire for Floriane is expressed predominantly through looking, and through the ways she initially acquiesces to Floriane's requests that she act as a cover for her clandestine meetings with her boyfriend François. Floriane disappears while Marie waits for her to return, so that Floriane's unseen parents will believe her to be out with Marie. When Marie tires of this scenario, she refuses to wait and Floriane confesses she has never had sex with anyone, though she has kissed many young men, and has been subject to unwanted advances from older men. Concerned that her sexually experienced reputation will be ruined, Floriane enlists Marie's help to lose her virginity. When Floriane goes to a nightclub, hoping to pick up a stranger for this purpose, it is Marie who rescues her from a potentially unpleasant encounter, knocking on the door of the car saying Floriane's father is waiting to pick them up. Rather than being annoyed, Floriane gratefully accepts Marie's help, and then asks if she will be her first.

Your Body Doesn't Know What to Do

Initially hesitant, Marie agrees to assist Floriane and by consenting to this act she acknowledges their affinity and the fluid nature of their relationship—Marie is more than a friend, but not quite yet a lover. The sequence where she helps Floriane dispose of her hymen is shorn of eroticism. There may be many reasons for this: it could be a gesture toward not sexualizing these young protagonists, a desire to protect the young actors from experiences they may not feel ready to embody on screen, alongside wrestling with the complexities of how one might ethically depict young teen protagonists and their sexual experiences. The atmosphere of this scene is emotionally charged, but not with desire. Just as Marie cannot find the words to articulate her feelings for Floriane, this scene shows us two girls attempting to navigate a culture that has no space and no language for this friendship that has become something more. The deployment of silence in this sequence is therefore worth examining in greater detail. I return to Sontag's ideas about silence in art and how it comes equipped with certain assumptions: "the most common, and dubious version of the notion of silence … invokes the idea of 'the ineffable'" (Sontag 30). This association immediately poses an interpretive problem for a sequence like this one in which girls are silent, as it suggests the opportunity to consider them as passive, erotic objects in the Mulveyan sense, or as otherwise docile and compliant bodies. What *Water Lilies* makes evident is that a concern with beauty that is read as always "available" in the figure of the alternately admired and despised Floriane underlines the problem of associating beauty and silence. Floriane, when she acts as the traditional Mulveyan object of the gaze, is subject to the whims of a patriarchy that reads her as already excessively sexual, erotically experienced, and as Joanna Walsh reminds us "a space for something to happen." Marie's presence here, her attentive gestures, and silent gaze introduce an alternative lens through which Floriane may be seen by others, and through which she may see herself.

Simon Shepherd's remarks on the concept of erotic silence are also pertinent here; he suggests that intensely silent mutual gazing within an artwork or performance space can be utopian, and that silence under these circumstances "guarantees that one is free from the disapproval of another, where that disapproval is the gaze or sound which shames the voyeur" (1999: 36). Shepherd's conceptualization of erotic silence captures the tone of this sequence and the texture of its silence. Here silence facilitates a space for exploration and experimentation between the two characters, who do indeed engage in some intense, silent mutual gazing and there are no words or other utterances that might otherwise imply shame. But this sequence is very different from the sex scenes that take place between adults in Sciamma's *Portrait of a Lady on Fire* or Joanna Hogg's *The Souvenir Part I* and *II*. In this moment of silence what passes between the two girls might be considered a consensual transaction that is free from shame and disapproval. This is, however, still a moment of initiation for both Marie and Floriane. For Marie this is an opportunity to be physically closer to Floriane, which is something she clearly desires but has been unable to fully articulate, yet she is also conscious that she is assisting Floriane toward her own freedom and self-actualization.

This sequence shows us an initiation for girls who have seemingly never touched themselves and who do not possess the language to discuss their bodies beyond how they appear to others. Marie appears grimly determined though still tenderly attentive in the task of penetrating Floriane with her fingers, while Floriane shuts her eyes and seems about to cry in pain (see Figure 14).

Marie looks at Floriane, but remains on top of the covers, fully dressed, while Floriane is under the covers, having only removed her underwear. This sequence also finds echoes in Leduc's *Thérèse and Isabelle*, where Isabelle performs a similar act on Thérèse, but where language takes the place of silence: "She was putting out the virgin eye. I was in pain: I was approaching freedom but I couldn't see what was happening" (58). Sophie Lewis's translation captures something of the similar tone of the sequence in Sciamma's film, its complicated

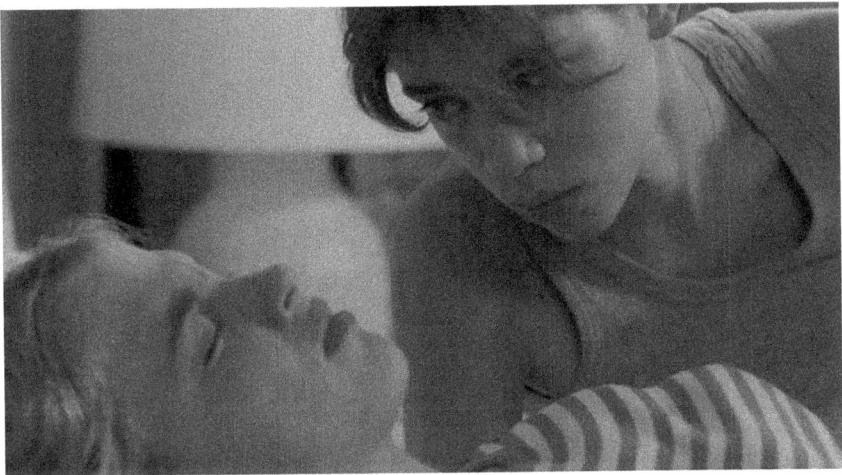

Figure 14 Floriane in discomfort as Marie (Pauline Acquart) inserts her fingers to help rid her of her hymen in *Water Lilies*.

desires, and illegible bodies. While Leduc's text is considerably more invested in conveying a breathless, mutual desire between her protagonists, the emotional complexity of this moment is important in *Water Lilies* when considering the shifting image of the silent girl and what her gaze means. Here, the gaze is both tender and confrontational, as Marie performs an act that lies somewhere between a duty of care and a gesture of desire.

Strange Delight: Unexpected Desires

The displays of swimming throughout *Water Lilies* offer opportunities for permission to gaze silently on feminine bodies, specifically for Marie to gaze at Floriane, and to begin to feel what Leduc calls "the octopus in the belly." This metaphor perfectly captures the ambivalence of unexpected desires—a sensation that may be pleasurable, or unsettling, much like the tone of the scene where Marie penetrates Floriane. This tone of persistent but uncertain desire characterizes the performances we see in *Water Lilies*. These uncertain moments of desire take place in the changing room, but also during practices, where Marie can observe the swimmers training underwater, and the complicated ways their legs move, which at times are filmed to evoke the movements of tentacles. Even though these swimming pool scenes are also tinged with shame and anxiety for Marie and Anne, both of whom are uncomfortable revealing their own bodies in the changing room, they nonetheless offer up sensual possibilities. This is reinforced by the kiss Marie and Floriane share in the pool changing room toward the end of the film.

While Floriane makes it clear she is heading back to the young men at the party, for Marie this is her moment of realization, the full expression of her queer girl desire. The film ends not with the promise of a successful romance, but with Marie and Anne floating together in the swimming pool. They are fully dressed, secure in a location where they have learned what it means to look and to be seen, and where they can continue their own friendship in a comfortable, mutual silence. They are set up in deliberate opposition to Floriane who is depicted dancing alone, with her eyes closed, but still surrounded by the surveyant gazes of her peers.

Water Lilies articulates a tension between girls who are perceived as physically mature, and those who are not, and the consequences of the various looks, stares, and gazes they encounter. For Anne, her seemingly adult body remains a source of confusion, and this is coupled with her awareness of feeling she is late to certain cultural milestones such as a first kiss. Anne expresses a desire to remain in the liminal place of girlhood, continuing her friendship with Marie where they play silly games, and enjoying the privileges of childhood. Anne is, at the same time, also curious about rites of passage and ends up having her first kiss alongside her first sexual intercourse, when her crush François turns up at her house. Driscoll comments, "The healthy body can equally provide a tyrannical body image in relation to which some girls (with different bodies) are coded as inferior or as manifesting insufficient attention and effort concerning their body" (253). This can certainly be applied to Anne's confusion about her own body in comparison to that of her peers. However, nowhere is this idea more perfectly illustrated than in the scene where a swim coach inspects her team before a competition, checking for body hair removal (see Figure 15). Girls are forced to stand with armpits exposed, in full make-up and matching swimsuits. But the coach is also inspecting the team to determine if any pubic hair is visible

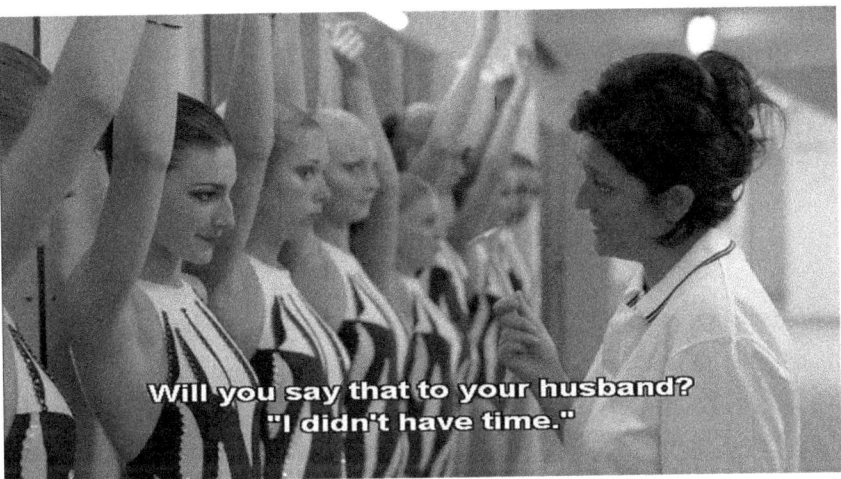

Figure 15 Another swim team is inspected for "tenue correcte" in *Water Lilies*.

beyond the boundaries of the swimsuit. One unlucky girl admits, "j'ai pas eu le temps/I haven't had time" and her coach admonishes her "c'est ça tu va dire à ton mari? J'ai pas eu le temps ?"

Here, failing to depilate the healthy body correctly is not connected to pool conditions or competition rules, but simply to patriarchal expectations of feminine bodily maintenance: "that's what you'll say to your husband? I didn't have time?" This scene reinforces the presence of the surveyant gaze as originating not just with men, but also with other women, and that this gaze extends well beyond judgment between adolescent girls. In this way, Marie's silent gaze acts as a nourishing, protective force for Floriane as it is the only space where Floriane is not subject to this kind of appraisal. That said, the film's conclusion implies that Marie finds a sense of belonging not through her kiss with Floriane, but through her rekindled friendship with Anne, when we see them floating in the pool, silently enjoying one another's company, the water fully supporting each of them. It is through mutual support and understanding, the feeling of being seen, understood, and loved that Anne and Marie can move forward, into a fuller understanding of the self. This recalls Dittmar's remarks that silence can indeed "encourage audiences to listen in new ways and discover new, *hitherto unsuspected modes of eloquence and assertion* [my emphasis]" (1994: 393–4). This mode is engaged by the final gestures made by Marie and Anne as they look up, out of frame, in a gesture that Sciamma will take even further in the ending she creates for Vic in *Girlhood*.

Bande des Filles/Girlhood

Girlhood/Bande des Filles begins with footage of an all-girls American football match. Here we see girls playing a powerful contact sport, and we hear their whooping, cheering and high-fiving at the end as the teams congratulate one another. As they walk home, entering the pathway to the housing estate, they become markedly silent, watched from the shadows by young men. The group thins as they peel off to their buildings. Marieme (Karidja Touré) is one of the last, walking alone to her door. Silence in the face of the male stare becomes a structuring concern of *Girlhood*.

Music and Silence in Girlhood

Where *Tomboy* and *Water Lilies* contain moments of contemplative or erotic silence and quietude in the absence of music, *Girlhood* (much like Ramsay's *Morvern Callar*) frequently fills up its moments of intensity with extra-diegetic soundtrack. The first of these moments occurs after Marieme has met the three girls whose gang she will eventually join: Lady (Assa Sylla), Adiatou (Lindsay Karamoh), and Fily (Mariétou Touré). When Marieme finds the pocket knife in amongst the kitchen dishes, we know it is significant, and she secrets the patriarchy's tool in her back pocket. The absence of dialogue that might discuss or articulate her decision to abandon domestic duty and join the gang signals the potential power of silence here, and the space it provides for significant gestures. Emma Wilson remarks of this film "it is with Touré, in their work together, in the images they produce, that Sciamma comes closest to being an ally to women of colour" (2021: 71). Even when words are exchanged in *Girlhood*, there are often ellipses that convey a world filled with rules that are unspoken, but clearly understood by the characters inhabiting this world.⁴ In this sense, the silences of *Girlhood* contain cultural expectations, just as they do in *Innocence*.

In her short story "The Company of Wolves," Angela Carter describes her adolescent protagonist as someone who "does not know how to shiver. She has her knife and she is afraid of nothing" (Carter 131). Here, the shiver evokes fear and the frisson of desire, a body not yet attuned to the snap of erotic attraction. This description also recalls Halberstam's shudder/shutter, the union of the listener and the viewer in horror cinema, and how the physical body can respond to fear or desire. In *Girlhood*, Sciamma offers her own narrative of what it means to lose your fear and find your shiver via the trajectory of Marieme (who later adopts the gender-neutral name Vic).

Space and *Girlhood*

Driscoll cites Cowie and Lees who introduce the idea of "'a bedroom culture and a lavatory culture' (28)" (258) to which girls are confined. "Most researchers contend, however, that girls make different use of private space than boys do" (Driscoll 26). Just as *Water Lilies* uses the space of the swimming pool and its changing rooms, as well as suburban bedrooms as locations where white femininity is constructed quite often in silence and via a variety of gazes, these are also spaces where a queer girl gaze is permitted to flourish, and *Girlhood* also explores how girls make different use of private and public space. In *Girlhood*, Black girls' bedrooms are not wholly private, as here they are often located in busy or oppressive family homes. As Wilson notes, this imagery has become part of the "unease about *Girlhood* as the work of a white French director, and Sciamma as an ally. Arguably the film does not go far enough in responding to and imagining the specific experience of being Afropean in contemporary France" (Wilson 2021: 66). This depiction of the

---

⁴ One such moment is Marieme's flirtatious exchange with Ismael (Idrissa Diabaté), where it's made clear they cannot date because he is friends with Djibril (who is involved in crime, but also authoritarian and abusive to his sisters). These rules are also evident in the sequence where Lady fights a girl from a rival gang, and the fight is clearly over once Lady's shirt has been removed.

home as a place of threat, particularly a place where patriarchal threat comes from within the family, has been criticized by Wilson and others in their re-evaluations of *Girlhood*.[5] We see Marieme/Vic experiencing the home as a space of both family duty and threat. She shares a bedroom with her middle sister Bébé (Simina Soumaré) and they are frequently tasked with the care of their youngest sibling, Mini (Chance N'Guessen). In an early scene, Marieme and Bébé joke about Bébé's developing breasts, but at the sound of male voices in the flat they instantly become silent. Marieme then tells Bébé not to tell their mother about her developing body, and to ensure she conceals her breasts from their older brother Djibril (Cyril Mendy). This early silencing in terms of the sudden halting of speech, and the interdiction to Bébé to keep her developing body a secret, indicates the various ways in which silence is deployed by girls here. Silence may be enforced by the potential threat of a male presence, but it is also a device for protection and prevention, a way of avoiding unwanted attention, even in spaces that are ostensibly private. This indicates that Sciamma's work is attentive to the different ways in which girls may make use of the bedroom, and the ways in which class and race may shift these uses. In *Water Lilies* the bedrooms of white, middle-class girls are presented as genuinely private, and are never shared or intruded upon unless by invitation. In *Girlhood*, poor, Black girls' bedrooms are shared, but only safe when they are purchased in a hotel. The exceptions to this are Ismael's bedroom which serves as a site of pleasure and refuge for Marieme/Vic, and later the bedroom that Vic occupies alone in a flat shared with their fellow grey economy workers.

Space only becomes something Marieme/Vic can navigate with confidence when they join forces with Lady, Adiatou, and Fily in the gang. As a group, the gang can successfully occupy public space in a variety of ways through fighting, dancing, and shopping. The group's use of private space is particularly interesting, since they regularly rent hotel rooms which they transform into their own, personal collective version of the "bedroom

---

[5] Sciamma has also acknowledged this in an interview with Elif Batuman in *The New Yorker* in 2022: "When asked which of her films looked the most different to her today, she replied without hesitation: "Girlhood." "It is problematic today," she said. Which means it was already problematic at the time."

and lavatory culture" Driscoll comments upon. The young women of *Girlhood* navigate the metropolis of Paris and its outlying communities, but as Black girls from the banlieues without large disposable incomes, they cannot access the landscape of the leisured flâneuse. The sequence where Marieme accompanies Lady, Adiatou, and Fily into Paris shows them strolling through shopping arcades with confidence, commenting to one another on what other women wear: leggings are passé, but another has a beautiful, expensive leather bag. The viewer never sees these commented-upon women and their clothes—they are only narrated to us via this surveyant girl gaze, a variation on the one we see that judges Floriane and that makes Anne and Marie judge themselves in *Water Lilies*. Dance is an important motif for space, visibility, and identity in *Girlhood*. Early in the film, the girls dance on the metro, encouraging Marieme to copy Lady's moves as she plays music off her phone. Scenes like this, which might be read as instances of nuisance to other (white) passengers, are configured as moments of bonding, and taking up public space in a way that renders the gang visible and powerful. Lindner's comments on the film confirm this reading:

> The girls variously re-appropriate and occupy public spaces that are not "meant" for them in these moments, through behaviours, appearances, and modes of taking up space that disrupt the normatively white, straight, patriarchal expectations and tendencies that normally shape these spaces and the bodies that occupy them.
>
> (236)

When they do wish to occupy private space, the girls are resourceful: they create intense fantasy spaces in anonymous hotel rooms where they bathe, chat, sing, try on clothes, drink, smoke, and dance. They have complete control of this space, and it proves an empowering one for them: they are free from harassment or run-ins with rival gangs, and can create spaces of pure personal, shared pleasure. This is evident in the careful attention Sciamma devotes to these sequences. The scene where Lady lipsynchs to Rhianna's "Diamonds in the Sky" is glamorously lit with a deep blue filter that compliments the girls' skin. Not only does this sequence and others like it incorporate twenty-first-century girls' ways of representing the self via smartphone photos and videos,[6] but the sequence evokes the lush camerawork frequently seen in music videos or luxury goods advertising.[7] The quality of these sequences also reinforces the difference between the culture of girls in *Water Lilies* and *Girlhood*. In *Girlhood*, the foursome support and encourage one another, and display a fierce loyalty. Lady in particular makes a profound intervention in Marieme's worldview which has a long-standing impact. Relaxing in the bath in a hotel, Lady watches a distressed Marieme debating whether to accept a call from Djibril. Lady orders her to switch off her phone and not answer. She then tells her "Faut que tu fasse ce que tu veux/you must do what you want" (see Figure 16) and makes Marieme repeat this phrase. She then bestows the "Vic" necklace, renaming her "Vic comme Victoire," a nickname for her new status in the gang, a girl who fights back, but also a gender-neutral name that will later remain as Marieme/Vic alters their appearance and their life (see Figure 17).

Figure 16 Lady (Assa Sylla) offers advice to Marieme/Vic (Karidja Touré) in *Girlhood*.

---

[6] The work of artists such as Kate Durbin and Amalia Ulman is of interest here, though it should be noted this is work carried out by artists who are both white women.
Kate Durbin "Hello Selfie" performances: https://vimeo.com/109163180
Amalia Ulman's Instagram performance "Excellences and Perfections": http://webenact.rhizome.org/excellences-and-perfections/20141014150552/http://instagram.com/amaliaulman
[7] An example of this is Rhianna's 2015 Dior advertisement: Rhianna for Dior Secret Garden IV https://www.youtube.com/watch?v=VsOtYffHbGg

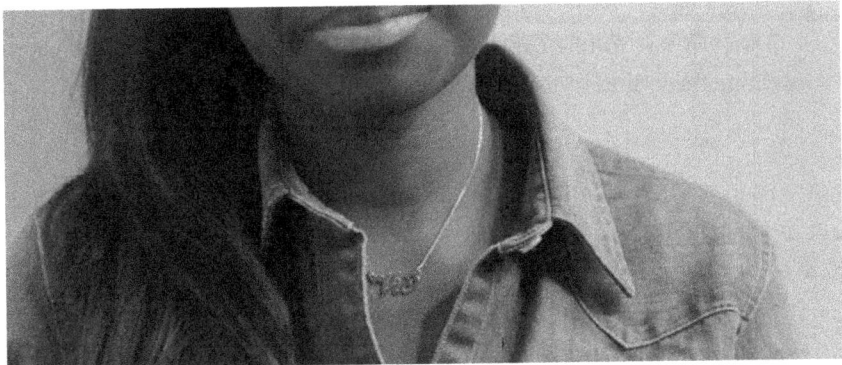

Figure 17 The "Vic" necklace in *Girlhood*.

Becoming "They": "je ne veux pas cette vie de fille bien"

In *Girlhood*, Sciamma deploys silence as a vehicle for Marieme/Vic's journey toward greater self-knowledge. Silence provides the opportunity to begin to look, to develop a gaze that sees the world and oneself in it. But, this is not just the curious gaze of childhood, this is a gaze that begins to assess how to put on and take off girlness and femmeness at will. Just as Laure/Mickael experiments with self-boying in *Tomboy*, so too does Marieme/Vic. Silence and slowness create this space: for looking, for listening, for bodies to take on new ways of being seen and this is corroborated by Vogelin's suggestion of a correlation between the self and silence: "the understanding of the self, born out of silence, politicizes the process of listening and the sonic subjectivity" (Vogelin 95). This suggests that silence can function as a radical space, and art that deploys silence can provide that space to the engaged spectator/listener.

This suggestion of radical space is present in the film, when Vic begins work as a drug dealer, and we see them deliberately moving between what So Mayer calls "high femme" (2016: 138 *Political Animals*) and gender neutral modes of dressing. For Lindner, this character's various forms of presentation remain evidence of an interest in representing fluid, queer identities just as Sciamma does with Laure/Mickäel in *Tomboy*:

> As with her other films, Sciamma refuses to tie her protagonist to a specific and fixed identity (is Marieme straight? bi? trans?), but acknowledges that

she is somehow "queer": "There are several ways to be queer: [Marieme] is really trying out the different identities that society has set for her. She is not inventing them, she's trying them out."

(2018: 226)

For Vic, moving around at night is part of work, and they have worked out a way to do this effectively. A blonde wig, make-up, a tight red dress, and black high heels are Vic's uniform for delivering drugs to a fancy party in an upscale Parisian apartment, populated almost entirely by white people. When we see Vic standing outside at night, they are dressed in loose, androgynous clothing. Later, we even see Vic has begun to bind their chest, something that Ismael, Vic's one-time boyfriend, asks about when he visits. We also see Vic flirting with Monica (Dielika Coulibaly), a woman who shares the flat and also works for Abou, the local gangster. All of Vic's colleagues are men, apart from Monica. Vic looks on, laughing as one of her older male colleagues harasses Bambi, a young Black girl on the estate that is part of the territory where they operate. Monica describes Vic as "tu joues l'homme/you're playing the man" but also asks "tu penses tu n'es pas une pute ?/You think you're not a whore?" indicating that to Abou, Vic is still very much a "pute" (see Figure 18).

The question of the meaning of the term *pute* here is particularly interesting. Despite being translated in the UK DVD subtitles as "bitch," the meaning of

Figure 18 Monica (Dielika Coulibaly) tells Vic they are still a "pute" in *Girlhood*.

"pute" is "slut" or "prostitute."⁸ This is the same word that Djibril uses to insult Marieme/Vic just before she quits the family home, when he is enraged at the discovery that they have had sex with Ismael. It is this reputation that leads Marieme to encounter Abou, and to go to work for him. Unlike Floriane in *Water Lilies*, Marieme/Vic has no ability to sneer, or to claim a sexually promiscuous reputation as something positive. In spite of the problem of being designated a "pute," Marieme/Vic's sexual encounter with Ismael is presented as chosen, consensual, and highly erotic. Ismael's ordinary bedroom is luxuriously lit with dark blue shadow, not unlike the "Diamonds" sequence, and takes on the same function accorded to the bedroom by Saidiya Hartman when she describes the revolution of intimate Black American life in cities in the early twentieth century: "The bedroom was a domain of thought in deed and a site for enacting, exceeding, undoing, and remaking relations of power" (2019: 61). After defeating a rival gang member in a fight, Marieme/Vic goes to Ismael's apartment. She enters his bedroom, waking him gently and tells him to undress, at which he wordlessly removes his vest. She urges him on, "encore [more or again]" and he removes his underwear. He lies in bed, waiting for her, and she strokes his back, pushing back the sheets to reveal his smooth bottom. In shadow, Marieme removes her hoodie—we never see her/their body. The atmosphere of this encounter is one which "depends on silence in order to experience that fragile extra-dailiness, something snatched from the mess of words" (Shepherd 1999: 38). Marieme/Vic gazes at Ismael, who in turn offers himself to his lover's gaze. Unlike the other men Marieme/Vic has encountered, Ismael is willing to make himself vulnerable, and the tender gestures of this scene indicate a shared, consensual act. This silence creates a space for these characters to consider new ways of being seen by one another and by the extra-diegetic audience, making the bedroom into the space evoked by Hartman's reading of archival evidence of Black American life. By offering a scene where Ismael is silent and acquiescent while still remaining a consenting, desiring participant, the space of his bedroom becomes a place of refuge from the violence and the imposed gender roles of the external world.

---

⁸ The Collins-Robert defines *putain*, the term from which *pute* is abbreviated, as "whore, hooker, hustler, slut" (769). I am grateful to Dr Elsa Bouet's comments and suggestions here as a native French speaker.

Here, Marieme/Vic can initiate this sexual encounter, Ismael can be passive, and he can offer his lover the gift of his desire.⁹

However, Monica's assertion that Vic cannot avoid being a "pute" in Abou's world proves to be correct, when Abou orders Vic to kiss him at a party later in the film. This takes place after Vic and Monica are slow dancing together. Although other people are also dancing, the pairing of Vic and Monica may be read as a kind of performance of potential lesbianism aligned with straight pornography. Hence when Abou appears, and orders Vic to kiss him, he is enraged when they refuse and slap him. It is never clear if Vic's flirtation with Monica might lead to something more. Knowing they have transgressed, Vic flees once more to Ismael's bedroom. He offers his home, marriage, the life of a "decent girl." But Vic gently refuses this, declaring "je ne veut pas cette vie de fille bien/ I don't want the life of a decent girl."

Once your protagonist has declared they no longer want the fairy tale, then where does that leave us? What does it mean to radically exit narrative convention? As can be seen in Figure 19, Vic hovers near the threshold of their old building, before gazing out at the city, and determinedly exiting the frame. With this gesture, Vic exits the gaze, silence, and binary gender. Vic has already left behind family, friends, and conventional femininity.

The absence of dialogue in these final moments suggests the radical possibilities of both silence and this threshold space, where a character who has already transitioned can now make a choice of where to go. Writing about the ending of *Girlhood*, Emma Wilson notes:

> As she slips out of the frame, the film shows blurred, tearful images of trees and tower blocks. But then Sciamma refuses that melodramatic moment. Marieme steps back in, dry-eyed, in focus, taking a breath, closing her eyes, about to run, or dive, into her future. She is suspended on the aching sounds of the Para One music. It is the start of a new day. Sciamma leaves Marieme's future unknown, radically unscripted. She lets the film dream. She leaves it in rapture.
>
> (2017: 18)

---

⁹ In her novel, *Passion simple*, Annie Ernaux's protagonist writes of her lover "il me fait cadeau de son désir/ he makes me a gift of his desire" (1991: 34).

Figure 19 Vic exits the frame at the end of *Girlhood*.

Just as *Water Lilies* ends with a strong sense of both solidarity and possibility, with Marie and Anne gazing upwards, *Girlhood* ends with the sense that its protagonist is heading into another story, and is now free from some of the constraints of patriarchal and heteronormative conventions.

3

Artist-Exhibitionists and Silence as Utopian Space in Lynne Ramsay's *Morvern Callar* and Joanna Hogg's *Exhibition*

Silence, when it is perceived as an inherently feminine quality, can make a person seem more like an object, or a symbol onto which fantasies can be projected. Silence connected to masculinity tends to be ascribed to a certain agency or profundity. These associations with autonomy or its lack also extend to bodies, particularly when they are more rigidly gendered and undressed. Men may remove their clothes before an audience and are perceived as retaining their autonomy, where women often remain objects, or at the very least their agency remains in doubt, as if we cannot believe a woman would voluntarily do this. Steve Neale (responding to Laura Mulvey's "Visual Pleasure and Narrative Cinema") once suggested that mainstream Hollywood cinema made no place for the male body as an erotic object (see Neale's "Masculinity as Spectacle"), and it would seem there are still few narratives that make space specifically for women's erotic agency. This presumption about lack of agency is deeply connected to our ideas of what it means to be a woman, or to be perceived as femme in public.[1] The legacy of the flâneuse, the woman who strolls and observes, and whether or not she can even exist, is particularly important when we consider the representation of women on screen, and the radical embodiment on offer in *Morvern Callar* and *Exhibition*. Just as silence creates fleeting moments of agency for Marieme/Vic in *Girlhood* and Marie in *Water Lilies*, I want to suggest that, following the work of Simon Shepherd, "silence—the space outside words—is utopian" (1999: 35) and that the silence

---

[1] As Hannah McCann, drawing on the work of Jack Halberstam, notes, "it is femininity that is the source of shame for both gay men (in their embodiment of the 'the sissy') and lesbians (in their 'failure to become properly feminine') growing up (2005: 226)" (2018: 83).

and quiet at work in both *Morvern Callar* and *Exhibition* create a utopian space of possibility in which desiring female agency can exist and flourish.

Rosalind Gill notes that women's sexual power in contemporary advertising tends to work in the following way:

> not by silencing or suppressing female sexual agency, but by constructing it in highly specific ways. Power works in and through subjects, less by modes of domination than through discipline and regulation ... Thus rather than agency or 'voice' being the solution to the silencing of women's desire identified by Fine and others, it becomes itself part of the apparatus that disciplines and regulates feminine conduct, that gets 'inside' and reconstructs our notions of what it is to be a sexual subject.
>
> (Gill 2008: 53)

What is useful here about Gill's argument is the idea of silence as the absence of narratives and representations of varied and authentic feminine desires. It can be difficult to trace narratives and spaces where women own their desires in ways that at the very least return the male gaze or, in some cases, operate outside it altogether (as Ciara Barrett has suggested in her discussion of Joanna Hogg's work). Gill suggests that while women may appear active and even vocal, the images on offer should not be automatically celebrated. Put another way, when the cacophony of the media landscape is just yelling at you about the right way to be sexy, silence becomes a powerful potential alternative. The films under discussion in this chapter portray silence in relation to female protagonists who exceed the figure of the flâneuse—Morvern Callar (Samantha Morton) and *Exhibition*'s D (Viv Albertine) are artist-exhibitionists with the ability to return and control the gaze.

The flâneuse

The flâneuse is an important predecessor to the artist-exhibitionist. Less frequently examined than her well-established male counterpart, Lauren Elkin's *Flâneuse: Women Walk the City in Paris, New York, Tokyo, Venice and London* goes some way to establishing and validating this figure. Elizabeth

Wilson cites the example of the popular nineteenth-century author Georges Sand (the nom de plume taken by Amantine Lucile Aurore Dupin; 1804–76) who was able to anonymously stroll the Paris streets "disguised as a man, she could experience the pleasures of being a *flâneur*—... 'no one knew me, no one looked at me ... I was an atom lost in that immense crowd'—an experience denied most middle class women" (Wilson 1991: 52). Sand used her literary success, and her wealth to openly flout convention in a number of ways, including regularly donning men's attire, and Janet Wolff correctly notes that Sand's experience and the fact that we have a record of her experience were unusual for the time. While Sand's habits were well-known, the experience she articulates depends on the privilege of being able to act as she wished, passing as male when convenient, and not being openly identified as the flâneuse, the specifically feminine iteration of the man of the crowd. Wilson also makes a fleeting connection between the sex worker and the possibility of the flâneuse in nineteenth-century Paris[2] when she notes that "the prostitute could be said to be the female flâneur" (55). There is a rich and varied history within fine art of depicting public women as associated with sex work: café dwellers, opera goers, dancers, flower sellers, barmaids, or laundresses have all carried this association. These static images represent an important record of how and where women appeared in public space, and they remain potent repositories for our cultural assumptions about what it means to be a visible woman in public. Images like Gervex's *Le Bal de l'Opéra* (1886) and Félicien Rops' *Buveuse d'Absinthe* (1865) show us a lexicon of style with regard to fashionable feminine dressing, implicitly posing a question to the viewer of what it means to "draw attention to oneself." The flâneuse, as she is represented in nineteenth-century European fine art, is more often than not both a fashionable woman and a potential sex worker. The legacy of this imagery should not be underestimated when it comes to the question of how women (or indeed any person who identifies as femme) navigate public space. These are the predecessors to the artist-exhibitionist figures we see embodied by Morton and Albertine.

---

[2] An idea I've written about elsewhere. See Artt, S. (2018). "Femme Publique": The brothel sex worker as anti-Flaneuse in the television series Maison Close. In M. Pietrzak-Franger, N. Pleßke, and E. Voigts (eds.), *Transforming Cities* (91–106). Heidelberg, Germany: Universitätsverlag Winter.

If we move forward, into the twentieth century Jean Rhys's work shows us the downbeat flâneuse of 1920s Paris. Unable to access Sand's euphoric joy, Rhys's protagonists are often uncomfortable: caught out by changes in weather, temporarily housed, or otherwise troubled, they roam the streets out of anxiety rather than choice. In the short story "In the rue de l'Arrivée,"[3] the protagonist Miss Dufreyne is followed in the street by a stranger: "a man was slinking up not quite alongside, a little behind her, cap pulled low over his eyes, … 'Mademoiselle' said the man, 'are you walking alone so late?'" (Rhys 1987: 53). Miss Dufreyne feels the penetrating gaze of the flâneur: "Those wary eyes had watched hundreds of women scold and sulk and sob and finally cry themselves into a beaten silence" (Rhys 54). While she feels as if the flâneur accurately perceives her emotional state, this does nothing to alter her miserable circumstances. Rhys's work represents an important intervention, articulating an instance of what it means to be seen by the flâneur, but to be unable to return the gaze on the same terms.

Contemporaneous to Rhys, the presence of the gazing public woman can also be found in the work of Colette. In *Chéri*, we note its handsome male protagonist is observed as he strolls through the streets of Paris: "The eyes of women followed his progress with silent homage, the more candid among them bestowing that passing stupefaction which can be neither feigned nor hidden" (1920: 79). These women cast their admiring glances at Chéri, and Colette clearly indicates that these gazes are not always furtive, but instead "candid" indicating a lack of shame that implies it was indeed possible for women to not only gaze at the flâneur, but appraise him in the way Baudelaire famously observes and appraises the woman in his poem "À un passante." This precedent established by Colette is significant when it comes to considering the artist-exhibitionist who creates her own auditory spaces and opportunities for collaborative, desiring gazes in *Morvern Callar* and *Exhibition*.

Deborah Parsons dares to ask, "Can there be a flâneuse and what forms might she take" (Parsons: 2)? Returning to the work of Baudelaire, the most frequently cited nineteenth-century male articulator of the *flâneur*, she notes,

---

[3] While there is no precise date for this story, Diana Athill clearly identifies the timeline for three groups of stories in her introduction to the Collected Short Stories. This story is clearly part of Rhys's early work, written prior to her first novel *Postures/Quartet* first published in 1928.

"All the women common to Baudelaire's work are observers, and through them it is possible to question the assumption of the masculinity of public space and to formulate the beginnings of the conceptual idea of a flâneuse" (Parsons 24). Rhys's and Colette's works come the closest to providing a sense of what the flâneuse's look might mean. Rhys excels at articulating the acute discomfort felt by women when they are watched by the flâneur. Colette, on the other hand, gestures toward what we might term a kind of interstitial gaze as she describes women gazing candidly on the charms of Chéri, who enjoys being admired in this way. Even Rhys's work contains flashes of this gaze. Early in her first novel *Quartet*, the following observation emerges, not entirely ascribed to any specific female character: "The Beautiful Young Men undulated ... they were spiteful and attractive and talented" (48). The presence of this observation suggests a gaze that is akin to the one acknowledged by Colette, an example of women looking at men, who may or may not be aware of how they are being observed. Colette and Rhys offer examples of what it means to gaze at the flâneur, a figure who may well be highly aware of or indifferent to those observing him.

The question of what it means to be a woman in public still looms, as does the potential agency of the woman's look, their awareness of others looking, and whether a shared, knowing gaze is possible. Joanna Walsh, in her autobiographical novel *Break.up*, observes: "A woman in the city is a space for something to happen: a girl alone at the table in the square looks like an opportunity, a location for an encounter, something that will change her, or the man who encounters her" (2018:125). While the sense of potential threat that tends to characterize Rhys's work is absent in this extract from Walsh, there is still the sense of woman as not self-contained. Others do not perceive her as capable of being alone with her own thoughts (though Walsh's novel is predominantly concerned with just this). Somehow, the solo woman must be asking for something in the way she looks. As Summer Brennan observes, "a woman is always seen to be *saying* something with her clothes, in a way a man is not" (Brennan 2019: 107). If we look back to Colette once more, we can see the resonance of Walsh's observation in *Chéri*. Eating with an old acquaintance in a noisy restaurant, Chéri casually asserts his seductive powers: "He forgot that very handsome young men ought to pretend indifference; he began to scrutinize the dark girl opposite, so that she trembled under his expert gaze" (1920: 82). Here, a woman, who may be alone or dining with someone else, is still open to Chéri's look because she is in a public space, a location for an encounter. What sets this apart is the way in which the affect of Cheri's "expert gaze" is described. What would it mean to have the woman describe this experience of being looked at? What sort of shiver is she experiencing? I wish to suggest that *Morvern Callar* and *Exhibition* take up this challenge through their articulation of the artist-exhibitionist to show us her thoughts, her experiences, and her look, whether she is a solo female traveler like Morvern, or a solo woman in urban space like D. The question of how women are permitted to be in public remains fraught with concerns around dress, personal safety, the right to be alone, and the right to possess the look or share a gaze.

Writing about her own experiences as an artist interested in the idea of the flaneuse, Helen Scalway notes, "The woman who strolls alone is still either a streetwalker or a stupidly naive victim who is just asking to be robbed" (Scalway 164). Considering her own experiences walking in London, she notes: "In order to stop safely, I have to buy space (in a cafe or cinema) or look as though I am at least a potential purchaser in a shop, or possess a pass to gain admission to a library, museum, club, etc." (Scalway 166). And yet, considering the experience of the girl in the restaurant who trembles under Chéri's desiring gaze, there is no guarantee that any of the spaces Scalway lists are places to stop safely. Certainly, no one wonders what a solo woman might be doing if she is in a café, cinema, library, or museum—the location itself provides a purpose. But she may still be perceived as "a space for something to happen."

In Lynne Ramsay's film *Morvern Callar* (2002), a quiet soundscape is established early. Morvern is first seen lying silently on the floor of her flat, next to the body of her dead lover. Immobilized with shock, a prolonged silence opens this film. This is a troubling silence, unsettling in its duration. Movement provides some relief, as we see Morvern tenderly caressing her partner's slashed wrists, an indication that this is a character who will not remain paralyzed by trauma. The silence is finally punctured as Morvern taps the keyboard of the computer, where James has left his suicide note and the manuscript of his novel. Shortly thereafter, we see her beginning to move around the flat, and around James's body. She begins, perhaps shockingly, to ready herself for a night out, and we see her applying eyeliner and nail polish, leaving her flat in a tight black dress and a heavy leather jacket. Morvern sets off into low-lit streets, but rather unusually there is no sense of menace here. Morvern walks at night without any sense of being on her guard. The silence of this brief sequence is not the tense hush of the crime or horror film, the silence from which we know the threat will emerge. This is the quiet of a rural housing estate, a quiet associated with nature and underpopulated areas. This comfortable, unthreatening silence is a texture that will characterize Morvern herself, who rarely speaks, and the silence she carries with her as she moves through the world. She soon meets her friend Lanna (Kathleen McDermott) who is waiting for her on a busier main road and the sound of traffic replaces the soothing quiet of Morvern's neighborhood. What is remarkable about these quotidian moments as we observe the two women on a night out is the absence of the kind of menace that tends to follow depictions of women walking at night.[4] Morvern and Lanna move through the world without being menaced because they have every right to be there—this is their town, their space. Ramsay presents us with the vision of what it means to confidently own public space and this is part of what renders Morvern's silence powerful.[5]

An earlier example of a film that places its female protagonist in similar scenarios is Carine Adler's *Under the Skin* (1997). Iris (also played by Samantha Morton) is a public woman who is simultaneously too sexual, and too odd when we see her walking through crowded city streets at dusk, clad in outfits that display her body: old slips, a fur coat, sunglasses, and ill-fitting wigs. Iris is certainly making a spectacle of herself, and this is something her co-workers remark on negatively in the film, describing her as both "a bit of slut" and her behavior as "sad." But for Iris, the bodily experiences she has in the wake of

[4] Even an immersive, binaural performance *Night Walk for Edinburgh*, staged during the Edinburgh Art Festival in August 2019, issued warnings to participants about personal safety and its video component contained numerous instances of the artist being peered at or intimidated by male passersby.
[5] In films like Agnès Varda's *Sans Toit Ni Loi/Vagabond* (1985) or Cate Shortland's *Somersault* (2004) its girl protagonists also walk at night, but they are girls on the run, they are girls in peril. Therefore, their sexuality, when it emerges, is always tinged with a sense of threat, something that is utterly absent from *Morvern Callar*.

her mother's death are the things which keep her tethered to the world. Her body and what it can feel, how it desires, is what matters here. Iris embodies an exhibitionist stance through both her clothing and her behavior: we see her openly return a passing man's appraising look before approaching him for sex, and we hear her talking frankly on the phone to an occasional lover about the kind of sex she would like them to have together. Like a number of texts that portray women who have sex with multiple partners, Adler's *Under the Skin* shows the "too sexual" woman engaging in behavior perceived as risky, because it involves the long-standing conflation between promiscuity, the woman in public, and the sex worker. Iris is indeed "a space for something to happen" since she is intent on picking up men for casual sex as a coping strategy in the wake of her mother's death.[6] Images like this are important in the sense that they retain a messiness that allows for greater complexity in terms of offering a wider range of female representation on screen, and this performance also acts as an important predecessor for the artist-exhibitionist. Yet, the association between trauma and women who have sex with multiple partners remains troubling. There remains a sense of being guilty, not just of being female in public, but of being a desiring female subject.

Just as Scalway notes that she must often at least pose as a customer to gain access to certain spaces if she wishes to stop safely, Iris deliberately cultivates an image that invites the gaze. She strolls in high heels, tight dresses, and her mother's old fur coat, knowing the response she will evoke when she is dressed "like a slut" as her sister tells her. Even Rhys's novels contain the seeds of this sense of being a target and being looked at. In *Voyage in the Dark* (1934), protagonist Anna Morgan notices how fashionable clothing works: "The clothes of most of the women who passed were like caricatures of the clothes in the shop-windows, but when they stopped to look you saw that their eyes were fixed on the future. 'If I could buy this, then of course I'd be different.' Keep hope alive and you can do anything" (Rhys 1934: 111). In Rhys's novel,

---

[6] Phoebe Waller-Bridge's *Fleabag* (first performed on stage in 2013; television adaptation 2016) depicts a protagonist whose sexual promiscuity is associated with unprocessed guilt and mourning over the death of her best friend. The BBC series *Wanderlust* (2018) depicts therapist Joy Richards (Toni Collette) as part of a couple who opt to explore non-monogamy. At the series' conclusion, her desire for intimate encounters with other men is partially ascribed to unprocessed guilt over a client's suicide.

there is a sense of not only how fashionable women are made conspicuous through their clothing, but this in itself grants them permission to be in public, strolling the streets and looking into shop windows, imagining their lives as different through the promise of fashion. This frequently configures the fashionable woman as in thrall to an unobtainable ideal, a spectacle to be looked at. Iris in *Under the Skin* refuses this image of the fashionable woman, deliberately constructing herself as a disruptive and unruly figure through her confusing dress, and frank sexual behavior. The men she approaches seem entirely unfazed by her distinctly odd clothing, and are glad to accept her sexual advances.

With these earlier images in mind, it is therefore crucial to examine just what it is that Lynne Ramsay does in *Morvern Callar* in terms of successfully portraying an artist-exhibitionist and a largely silent but nonetheless active and collaborative gaze. As Lanna and Morvern enter their local pub on their night out together, they stand out in their tight dresses and make-up, in contrast to the rest of the customers who are unremarkably clad, despite the presence of tawdry decorations indicating a half-hearted attempt at Christmas cheer. As Lanna and Morvern are greeted by regulars and work colleagues, they settle in for a few drinks. Lanna establishes eye contact with some young men, thoroughly confident in her appeal; Lanna knows that the secret to non-verbal flirting is simply to look back and hold that shared gaze. She and Morvern are soon in a car driven by these same young men, on their way to a bacchanalian house party. These brief sequences with Lanna's frank and playful gaze recall the candidness of Colette's women gazing after Chéri, but Lanna is the one dictating the terms here, her gaze is the initiator, and the men meet her gaze. Lanna's gaze is bold, but it is not quite the sexual directness displayed by Iris in *Under the Skin*. This is perhaps because Lanna's gaze is distinctly portrayed as flirtatious, and it is clearly reciprocated by the young men she selects. Lanna's gaze secures access to further adventure and we see both her and Morvern laughing and leaning out the windows of the car, as the young men drive them to the party.

It is during this party that we see another instance of what we might term Morvern's instinctual ownership of space. Just as she has set off earlier from her flat, unafraid and unconcerned because she is in entirely familiar territory, she wanders outside the house where the party is taking place and stands on the shore in darkness. A passing boat shines a high-beam light onto her and she lifts her skirt. Though Ramsay films Morvern at a distance in a long shot (see Figure 20), we can see Morvern lift her chin in a gesture that is both defiant and provocative. She too displays a candid, frank gaze here. Is the raised skirt an invitation—come over here? A provocation—you can't catch me? She is, recalling Walsh's words, "an opportunity for encounter" but it is very much on her terms. She has not paid to access this space, and has taken ownership of it through her presence and her gestures. Morvern's familiarity with her surroundings has given her the confidence that enables her exhibitionist identity.

Throughout this party sequence, we see Morvern and Lanna engaging in behaviors that would be the prelude to tragedy in other narratives: dancing unselfconsciously, chatting to strangers, drinking and taking drugs, and having group sex. Yet, all of these experiences are depicted as not only harmless, but actively pleasureable and consensual for both women, with no kind of punishment ensuing. This is part of what makes *Morvern Callar* so radical—it revels in the possibility of pleasure and intimacy for women without negative repercussions. It suggests that women can, in fact, own the gaze, and that they

Figure 20 Morvern (Samantha Morton) raises her skirt while standing on the river bank in *Morvern Callar*.

can achieve erotic agency in relation to their own self-presentation. Ramsay lets us imagine, through Morvern and Lanna, what it would be like to move through the world without fear and to occupy that space of utopian, erotic silence.

A new, radical intimacy and the space for the gaze of the artist-exhibitionist are further established the next morning, as Morvern and Lanna make their way back from the party. They walk along the road together, utterly without shame in their high heels and laddered tights. They stop off to visit Lanna's grandmother, and to get warm. Here, we are shown the tender scene of Morvern and Lanna sharing a bath together. The two women are not prudish or self-conscious with each other, and the scene's ambiance evokes childhood, where a bath might be shared with a sibling or close friend, not unlike the bathing scenes we see in Sciamma's *Tomboy*. Yet, the fleeting scene at the party that shows Morvern and Lanna in bed together with one of the young men creates a sense of ambiguity, a reluctance to name the nature of their friendship explicitly. Lisa Johnson confirms this queer reading: "With this friendship that is not sexualized and intimate only in bounded ways … her [final] proposition to Lanna [at the film's conclusion] can neither be called lesbian or *not* lesbian" (2004: 1368–9). Morvern and Lanna's friendship contains the potential for erotic intimacy, much like Marie and Floriane in *Water Lilies*, or Vic and Monica in *Girlhood*. This absence of categorization is a fascinating instance of silence in the sense of not verbalizing or naming something. While this not-naming might be read as erasure, in the context of *Morvern Callar*, it indicates a potential comfort with the idea of not needing to conform to expectations, or indeed to give something a name when it is not required.

One of the key ways in which Morvern is presented as artist-exhibitionist is through the way in which she maintains and curates her own personal aural space. Morvern's perpetual headphones feel very predictive of how, within only a few years, this would become many people's default position with the advent of ipods and smartphones and the ability to carry and access an ever-larger personal library of music. To be enveloped in a perpetual aural cloud of your own selection is no longer in any way unusual. For Morvern, this is a way of curating her own soundscape long before the advent of music streaming services and ear pods made this ubiquitous behavior. In the era prior to music streaming, with a collection that spans the formats of vinyl, CD and cassette, Morvern must create cassettes with playlists that take time and effort to produce, in order to have a portable range of music at her disposal. At the time the film is set, this form of musical curation takes far more effort and technical ability, and demonstrates a desire to exercise and present taste culture and can be read as an early example of Morvern's artistic practice. While she is clearly comfortable with silence and quiet, particularly when it comes to not feeling the need to fill it with small talk, or even the urge to continuously share and discuss feelings, she nonetheless takes great care in selecting music that is obscure and unexpected. Nowhere is this more significant than in the scene where she dismembers James's body in the bathroom while listening to *The Velvet Underground*'s "I'm Stickin' With You." The grim task and Morvern's stoic expression throughout are contextualized by the presence of this track, with its tender, child-like lyrics executed by Lou Reed and Maureen Tucker. The clearly discernible lyrics convey a sense of devotion that encompasses the radical, collaborative intimacy displayed by Morvern and Lanna, and suggests that this also extends to James.

As Morvern dismembers James to this soundtrack, the atmosphere becomes tender and moving rather than just grisly and bizarre. Just as no one can have access to the truth of their relationship, Morvern ensures that James's death remains intimate and private. She takes sole responsibility for his body, burying him in the wilderness, accompanied by gestures of profound joy and communion with nature. Rather than a sinister silence, Morvern fills up the space that might be filled with tears or inadequate platitudes with music she has selected that speaks of her feelings of devotion when she cannot or does not want to find the words to do so.

Once the action moves to Spain, we observe Morvern moving through a nightclub with her headphones in. In the bathroom, Lanna chats with two young men, while Morvern remains silent, drinking water, taking it all in. She returns alone to the hotel, and we see her observing the revelry from the privacy of her balcony. While there is noise from other guests as they carouse, it is perceptible as being at a distance. Here, Morvern occupies the position of an observer. Just as she seems to wander around the club, observing but not really participating or interacting with anyone, none of the things happening at the resort really seem to touch her.

For Johnson, part of *Morvern Callar*'s power stems from its use of a "lowered gaze" (Johnson 1368) which is sometimes also a "shamed gaze [that] seems itself to produce new interest" (1368). While I appreciate this theorization of the depiction of the shamed gaze, I do not entirely agree with Johnson in relation to where and when this gaze might appear in *Morvern Callar*. This lowered gaze is, however, a pertinent description in relation to the film and how it allows for a new angle on women's experience. Johnson comments on how Morvern's lowered gaze allows her to notice and follow a cockroach, which leads her into the hallway and toward another room, where she encounters a young man who has just learned of his mother's death. "Stay if you want and talk to me," he says. They cry, dance, and have sex. But, the sex they have together is not wild, holiday sex but something less easy to categorize, it seems to be more about a short-cut to establishing intimacy, a way of making it okay to move past boundaries and in this sense it is much closer to the sexual encounters we see in *Under the Skin*. This too is part of *Morvern Callar*'s display of a radical intimacy that encompasses friendship, compassion, and eroticism in encounters that remain beyond easy designation—they exist unnamed and undefined in a utopian, erotic silence. The artist-exhibitionist creates the spaces for these encounters through their curated silences, and bodily gestures. Johnson suggests that the intimacy of this particular encounter between Morvern and the young man "produces not romance but perhaps an even more intense shame response. When she wakes in the stranger's embrace, Morvern panics at the intimacy …" (1368). While I acknowledge the validity of this interpretation, I would like to argue for another possible reading here. There seems to be an affinity established between the two characters when Morvern says to him, "I can tell you about my foster mother's funeral if you like." Other than that, we never get to hear what they say to each other, though the sequence shows them talking to one another without access to their dialogue. They cry, talk, laugh, and fuck but whatever else these characters share remains theirs. Just as we never have access to Morvern's relationship with James prior to his death, the full extent of her connection with the man at the resort remains veiled but still worthwhile.

After this encounter, Morvern becomes the artist-exhibitionist in earnest. Dragging Lanna away from the resort, they take a faintly surreal taxi journey. The taxi goes where Morvern tells it, exploring at random until they reach a village in the hills. Morvern and Lanna eventually end up wandering through an agave field and here their different views on their surroundings are established. Morvern observes "Wow, this is amazing" while Lanna is dismissive and annoyed: "This? It's the middle of nowhere." Morvern is unfazed by being alone in the countryside, and being compelled to silence through her lack of Spanish presents no difficulty. Yet, she manages to navigate the landscape by gently pointing, and by relying on a shared understanding of facial expressions and other gestures, such as when we see her quietly share an understanding glance with the waitress in a café as they both observe a group of older men singing and showing off. The waitress makes a gesture at the side of her head, rolling her eyes, clearly referring to the group of older, Spanish men. Morvern smiles at this shared gaze, where the experience of being women observing male behavior overrides the need for a verbal exchange. This shared gaze is significant, as it marks out another instance of women exchanging a feeling while watching men, observing their behavior but without a view to anything else.

Later, we see Morvern trying on a new, flowered, halterneck dress in her hotel room and langorously painting her nails looking out at the sea. Here, she seems to have seized on the idea that she cannot just dream of being different the way that Rhys's passing women do when they look at clothes in shop windows; Morvern can achieve this difference. Dressed in her new attire, Morvern becomes an artist when she takes on the mantle of novelist. When Morvern meets her London publishers, they praise her novel's "distinctive female voice." This is of course a great joke, since they interpret Morvern's taciturnity as artistry or even shrewdness. Her silence when they begin to discuss money prompts them to offer her £100,000 for her manuscript. The fact that the novel has been written by her dead partner, and she has only put her own name to it, suggests that there is an interchangeability between the author's voice—the book is now hers in every sense, to do with as she wishes. Or perhaps to suggest Morvern has contributed to this work in ways that the film does not show. Perhaps she is claiming back what belongs to her, since in his suicide note James writes he has written the novel for her. If Morvern is the muse, in the same way as Baudelaire's *passante* provides an inspirational figure, then perhaps this work belongs more to Morvern than we might initially have imagined. Morvern's final moment of transformation comes when she takes the publishers with her into a graveyard. Morvern's pace here is purposeful, as if she has visited this location before. Her publishers look on in silence as she pauses before a small altar, holding a flower and righting a figurine that has fallen over. Morvern is shot in profile, on the left side of the screen, and the camera pans to then reveal her on the right, as if she has just seen her double. This moment of quiet performance cements Morvern as an artist-exhibitionist, ready to dazzle her audience, in touch with a mysterious, secretive, creative force. The breaking of the 180 degree rule here serves to underscore this transformation. After this, she returns briefly to Scotland to collect her cheque, some records, and to try and entice Lanna to join her on her travels. But Lanna is still tied to geographic place, and not even Morvern's radical declaration, "fuck work, Lanna" can uproot her. Morvern sets off alone once more, into the night and free in her new identity.

Exhibition

In her memoir about choosing not to become a mother, Sheila Heti writes: "There is something threatening about a woman who is not occupied with children. There is something at-loose-ends feeling about such a woman. What is she going to do instead? What sort of trouble will she make?" (2018: 32). If the trouble Morvern makes is the rejection of shift work in favor of creative and sexual freedom, then Joanna Hogg's *Exhibition* offers up a different but related set of images of women in public and private space. While the urban stroller or traveling woman does not feature as frequently here as in *Morvern Callar*, *Exhibition* nonetheless provides evidence of a woman with her own active gaze, one that is often showcased through textures of silence, and in spaces that blur the boundaries between the domestic and the city street.

D and her partner H (Liam Gillick) inhabit a large, modernist house. The house is so large that they often communicate with one another via an internal telephone system, speaking from their respective offices. Where Morvern moves from an exhibitionist stance to incorporate an artist identity through silent practices, D begins the narrative already established as an artist, and whose exhibitionist aspects are slowly revealed and incorporated into her work.

Throughout the film, D is seen making art and going about her everyday activities in silence. She frequently rehearses for bodily performances that make use of props of various kinds and that involve manipulating her body through costumes made of underwear, tights, translucent fabric, and plastic tape. In addition to these processes, we also occasionally see D drawing, but we are never shown the drawings, as opposed to her process of planning bodily performances. These rehearsals and experiments are always carried out in silence in the sense that it is not sound-tracked with intra- or extra-diegetic music and there is no dialogue or voiceover. Much of D's work is undertaken in her home office, behind a set of horizontal blinds. The window in her office faces a street in London, but the blinds ensure she is not always visible unless she wishes to be. D is sometimes prompted to look into the street, particularly if she perceives some kind of accident or altercation is taking place, but otherwise she is focused on her own art-making.

As an older woman (at the time the film was made, Albertine was in her late fifties), D might be presumed to have aged out of being too frequently noticed when she goes into public space, or even when she invites the gaze into her own artistic space. However, the fact that D is played by the exceptionally beautiful Viv Albertine problematizes this assumption. D's work as a performance artist who uses her own semi-clothed or nude body makes her into a particular kind of spectacle. One of the ways in which the boundaries between private and public urban space are blurred in the film is through the use of the blinds which cover the window of D's office.

The horizontal blinds that cover the street-facing window of D's office are used in a number of sequences. Coming toward the fruition of planning a performance, she is seen rifling the blinds up and down with her hands, as she kneels in front of them while nude. This sequence is a puzzling one: it is unclear whether this is something that may become an aspect of a later performance, or whether it is yet another expression of D's polymorphous sensuality, something which is displayed throughout the film and which

Figure 21 D (Viv Albertine) rifling the horizontal blinds on her office window, as seen from the street.

feeds into her work. This includes taking pleasure in nude, solo swimming, masturbation, and practicing restorative yoga poses around the house.

The ambiguous nature of this sequence with the blind recalls the similarly hard-to-define moment in *Morvern Callar*, where Morvern raises her skirt on the river bank, while a passing boatman shines a high beam of light onto her in the dark. The silence of these sequences is constructed by the women themselves—there is no intra- or extra-diegectic music, and there are no fetishizing close-ups. We see their bodies at a distance, but agentic in their gestures. Morvern raises and lowers her skirt, and D rifles the blinds to reveal and conceal glimpses of her figure (see Figure 21). Like Morvern, D is filmed from a distance, outside the house. She is behind glass, and while we glimpse flashes of her nudity, she too remains mysterious, daring, and in control of what others can see through her use of the blind. Here too, D's ambiguity remains intact, and we are unclear as to the precise function or purpose of this action. Is it part of the performance or part of D's sexual expression? Or both? Like Morvern, D presents us with a reclaiming of exhibitionism as a position, and a sexual identity. This doesn't limit the ways in which these actions also feed into D's artistic practice, but it is also worth acknowledging the radical possibilities present in these sequences, and how they tap into Shepherd's ideas about erotic silence as space of collaboration, free from disapproval. This also gestures toward Johnson's reading of *Morvern Callar*'s lowered gaze, but supports my reading that that film presents a candid and collaborative gaze free from shame and suggests radical possibilities for new forms of intimacy, something that is further reflected in Sciamma's *Portrait of a Lady on Fire*. These sequences with the blind as a veil for D's naked body also suggest a gaze free from shame, though perhaps slightly less candid than the gaze that operates in *Morvern Callar*. D's control of the blind is more like the gazes of women that trail Colette's Chéri through the Paris streets—they do not meet his gaze, but he is their object. D does not meet any particular diegetic look, but perhaps that is the point. D's actions are ones that convey a desire to be seen and she occupies the position of both creator of a viewing event and the object of that event. Like Ramsay, Hogg is also interested in exploring what it means to move through the world without fear, though her vision is tempered by D's apprehension at the unpredictable nature of the urban environment (epitomized by her anxiety at H's decision to take a late night walk through their neighborhood). Where Morvern is clearly at home everywhere, D carefully creates and navigates certain spaces which become locations of erotic and artistic freedom and possibility. As Shepherd notes:

> So too, the erotic silence is very different from the activity of mere watching in silence, as an audience of dance does, because here the silent watching is in effect a form of reading … The erotic silence invites an audience into a space which does not require reading … in the erotic silence, the audience, the readers, are looked back at by the object that should be readable. The look back at the audience begins to produce the condition of mutual inspection, where we are uncertain if the other person is offering herself for us or looking to see if we are suitable for her.
>
> (Shepherd 1999: 37)

The ambiguity and sense of equality suggested by Shepherd fit well with the sequences in both *Morvern Callar* and *Exhibition*. Shepherd also mentions the work of Marina Abramović, and Adele Senior, Simon Kelly, and Lydia Brawner all comment on the role of silence in relation to the much discussed idea of "charismatic space" in Abramović's performances and whether her

2010 performance piece "The Artist Is Present" achieves this. Senior and Kelly suggest that the space where this performance took place is highly structured, and therefore far less free and utopian than the erotic silence Shepherd describes. However, we might consider whether *Exhibition*, in its portrayal of D, is successful in suggesting what an erotic silence might look like as part of both artistic practice and sexual expression.

Toward the end of the film D's workspace is fully revealed to us. She pushes back a series of sliding, pocket doors that we've seen her rush in and out throughout the film. This reveals an open space, clearly connected to her "office" but this space contains a large full-length mirror, floodlights, and various stools. D opens the blinds fully before beginning to costume herself in fishnet tights, black underwear, a sheer top, and she puts reflective tape around her torso in horizontal stripes. She wears a make-shift veil on her head. As she stands on a rotating stool, her hands on the ceiling, H watches her through the blinds from the dark street, taking up the position of the camera in relation to the sequence where she flutters the blinds. Only this time, we clearly see D looking down on H, from inside her workspace. She looks at him briefly, and continues turning herself around on the stool, before stepping down and calmly, confidently exiting the space, like an actor leaving the stage.

D's successful execution of this performance suggests she is able to command and marshal a shared gaze within the space she has created as artist-exhibitionist. Throughout *Exhibition*, we are confronted by the title, which clearly alludes to a display of an artist's work, as well as D's exploration and display of her own body. Here, D's body is her desiring instrument, and her art practice uses her body as a site of performance. D is exhibiting her body and herself in a way that blurs the boundaries between the internal, domestic space of the house and the external public space of the city and the street. It is telling that the boundaries of the house itself are not always readily apparent, in a scene where a man has parked his car in front of their garage, causing H to become enraged. The other man cannot see that this is part of the exterior of a private residence. This sequence might be interpreted as analogous to the way that women walking in the street are deemed to be open to comment, their boundaries not clearly discernible to other people. The blurring of these public and private thresholds is also evident in the sequence with the blind, and in the final revelation of D's performance. What is radical about D as artist-exhibitionist is that she is able to fully command her gaze, her spaces, and her silence.

Exhibition seems to be implicitly exploring an idea articulated by Hélène Cixous in "The Laugh of the Medusa" when she writes of "a woman's body with its thousand and one thresholds of ardour" (1976: 885) and how this concept helps to account for the synergy of D's bodily sensuality and her art practice. In addition to the key moment with the blind, we are also privy to a number of D's dreams and fantasies, which she narrates and records using a Dictaphone, and which are then offered in visual fragments. These instances clearly combine D's sensations of physical, sexual desire with a desire to be seen, heard, and understood in terms of her artistic work. This tension also characterizes her day-to-day relationship with H, who is also an artist of some kind, but whose work is not showcased in the film. D's masturbation is performative in the sense that it includes a costume and certain props. In the darkened bedroom, she wakes up and puts on black lace panties and heeled sandals. She rubs oil on her torso and masturbates. She orgasms, smells her fingers, and sighs with contentment. She slowly stretches out her legs and pulls the duvet back over herself, switches off the light, and goes back to sleep. All the while, H has been sleeping next to her, oblivious. In spite of the fact that the film audience witnesses this act of masturbation, the atmosphere within the film preserves this as a private ritual, and the sense that this is very much part of D's solo sexual expression, that this performance is only for herself and does not require anyone else. Yet, the way she reveals glimpses of her body with the blinds suggests she may be experimenting with the idea of having an audience. The sequence in the bedroom where D masturbates evokes Shepherd's notion of the space free from disapproval, a space that is very much at work in both *Exhibition* and *Morvern Callar*, where the filmmakers are clearly concerned with the portrayal of a space for women to move through the world not just without fear, but being able to experience desire and pleasure without negative repercussions. In fact, we might consider whether D's masturbation is a kind of ultimate solo performance. To show this being done by a woman in her fifties (albeit a very conventionally attractive one, with a slender, youthful body) is particularly transgressive, since women in mid-life are rarely accorded any kind of sincere sexuality on screen and Hogg's work remains a rare exception.

Throughout *Exhibition*, we witness an interweaving of D's experiences of solo bodily pleasure, her sometimes ambivalent response to sex with H, his desire to discuss her work and her refusal of this, combined with what for me emerges most strongly in the film: her desire to be seen, understood, represented, and loved as an artist and as a woman. Ciara Barrett also remarks on this complex relationship:

> The implication is that D's experience of her domestic environment is highly physicalised, even sexual. Indeed, it appears D is most interested in sexual situations and/or sex with her husband when she may be viewed in private from a public vantage point, taking in the full physical extent of her actions-as-performance.
>
> (Barrett 2015: 9)

Barrett's reading of D's relationship to space and sex resonates with my designation of her as artist-exhibitionist. This is a tension that has also been explored by Sally Potter in her landmark work *The Tango Lesson* (1997), which deals explicitly with this overlap of the personal and the professional. In *The Tango Lesson*, we see a relationship develop between Sally (Potter, playing a version of herself) and Pablo Verón (Verón, playing a version of himself), the dancer with whom she is making the film *The Tango Lesson*. In the film, Potter explores what it means for the director and her star to be intimately involved, where they are both working together and acknowledging the erotic frisson that exists between them. At one point in the film, they explicitly discuss their mutual decision to attempt to sublimate their attraction to one another into the creative work they are making together, deliberately acknowledging the energizing tension that can come from this kind of mutually agreed collaboration where desire is a powerful undercurrent. This exploration of the way in which life sometimes becomes art, the action-as-performance, is not often accorded to women, and therefore it is worth highlighting how a film like *The Tango Lesson* acts as a predecessor to *Exhibition*.

In *Exhibition*, this tension between work and the personal is also displayed in the scene where we see D on the phone discussing how she has been working in an "insular way" but also acknowledging that work has to be seen at some point. She's excited and pleased about this call, which is clearly the invitation to do a solo exhibition. After she finishes the call, she sits pensively for a few moments before ringing H on the internal extension to ask "do you still love me?" to which he replies, very tenderly "of course I do." This is followed by an elaborate fantasy sequence, overlaid with the film's only instance of diegetic music. D imagines herself attending an artist's talk where she is both the audience and the artist being interviewed. In some ways, this display of D on the stage and sitting in the audience parallels the doubling of Morvern in the Spanish graveyard, signaling a significant moment of transformation where the artist-exhibitionist fully materializes. Here, H is acting as interviewer and mentions what he sees as key aspects of D's work, namely "unpacking the domestic" and "place." She reiterates her refusal to discuss her work with him, "I don't want your judgement," she declares. H seems to feel that this diminishes his role in their relationship, whereas D seems content with the statement that H is her "companion" but not a critic or collaborator. Part of the film's drama derives from D's desire to maintain her art practice and her individual erotic life as distinct from her marital relationship, in spite of the fact that both D and H work at home, in a very large house, with ample space for two offices, and a great deal of opportunity for quiet contemplation. While D wants connection, she does not want all of her life to become art.

Both these films draw on a history of women in public, which includes the legacy of the flâneuse. In both of these films, the artist-exhibitionist and the (often silent) space she creates and occupies become vital for personal growth and freedom. For Morvern, it is travel and money that allow her to declare with total confidence "fuck work" and to pursue her own pleasures. For D, what is important is the space to create without judgment or time constraint, to explore the full range of her art practice and her sexuality. Both Morvern and D do not discuss their creative impulses with a partner, and while they seek collaboration, they do not always want this to go alongside long-term domestic partnership. These narratives show us the radical possibilities of artist-exhibitionists as figures who can create spaces of intimacy and creativity, free from fear and shame.

4

Sinister Silences and Mothering in Lynne Ramsay's *We Need to Talk About Kevin* and Lucile Hadžhalilović's *Evolution*

In Lynne Ramsay's *We Need to Talk About Kevin* (2011) and Lucile Hadžhalilović's *Evolution* (2016) we are faced with particularly challenging, uneasy images of motherhood. In these films, motherhood is depicted as a state of ambivalence, when it is not downright sinister. These are stories about bad mothers, or in the case of the women in *Evolution*, one might refer to them as mothers-who-are-not since while they care for the boys on the island, their interest in them is distinctly less about survival. Yet, neither of these films can be easily classed as horror—we are not in the territory of the monstrous mothers of *The Brood* (Cronenberg, 1979) or *Hereditary* (Ari Aster, 2018). One of the tragedies of *We Need to Talk About Kevin* is that the protagonist Eva (Tilda Swinton) begins as the ultimate flâneuse: a cosmopolitan travel writer and city dweller, who is trapped by maternity, lured to the suburbs, and punished with permanent notoriety as the mother of a teenage killer. At one point, we overhear an exchange between Eva and her partner Franklin (John C. Reilly), shortly after their son Kevin is born, where Franklin exclaims: "Ecuador? For three months?" Eva never undertakes this journey, evidently guilted into remaining behind.

In her memoir which deals largely with choosing not to become a mother, Sheila Heti writes of the trouble that might be made by women who don't have children. The trouble Eva makes in *We Need to Talk About Kevin* is, of course, the malevolent boy she makes with her body. Barbara Creed notes "the belief that mothers create monstrosities through the power of their imagination has a long tradition" (Creed 1993: 45) and in *We Need to Talk About Kevin*, this is coupled with Tilda Swinton's performance as the frustrated Eva, and Ezra Miller's sinister, disturbing portrayal of the teenage Kevin, a young man who commits an act of domestic terrorism. Rather than continuing to travel the world, building her business, and experiencing visceral pleasures such as those of La Tomatina (the bacchanalian tomato festival that begins Ramsay's film) *We Need to Talk About Kevin* is a portrait of a person trapped by biology, a conceit that also characterizes the pregnancy and birth that we see in Hadžhalilović's *Evolution*. In *Evolution*, the trouble made by women is the covert experiments conducted on the boys of the island, leading eventually to Nicolas (Max Brebant) giving birth to alien twins. Even though all the women we encounter in this film are ostensibly occupied with children, the women themselves are an unsettling presence despite their status as mothers, doctors, or nurses. Nicolas senses this disturbance, and when he sees the women on the beach at night engaging in a kind of cephalopodesque ritual, his suspicions are confirmed: these people are not entirely human, and their care-taking function cannot be taken for granted. In both these films, to be a mother is portrayed as something alien, otherworldly, and not particularly desired, but it is also a role that is so culturally revered that when you do it badly (or not at all) you run the risk of social exile.

Ramsay's film begins with a dark, empty house, a setting that makes us feel as if we are watching a horror movie (and of course, in a way, we are). We hear the sound of a sprinkler, and faintly, the sound of voices shouting in sequence. A fade to white takes us to a wide, overhead shot of a crowd of bodies, all tinted by some kind of red goo. As the camera draws closer, this is revealed to be the La Tomatina festival, but it is shot as if it is a bloody mob surging through the streets. As can be seen in Figure 22, Eva appears ecstatic, held aloft by the crowd, and then lowered into a pool of blood red tomato pulp. The low-level roaring of a crowd is punctuated by faint sounds that could be gunshots, followed by a woman's incoherent screaming. The soundtrack clearly doesn't belong to the visuals here, but suggests the kind of subconscious connection found in dreams. This dialogue-free opening sequence recalls the powerful opening of *Morvern Callar*, where Morvern initially appears to be reclining next to another person, bathed in a warm, golden light that flashes on and off. These few moments of what appears to be a tender intimacy are ruptured after the film's title is revealed, and we see Morvern lying on the

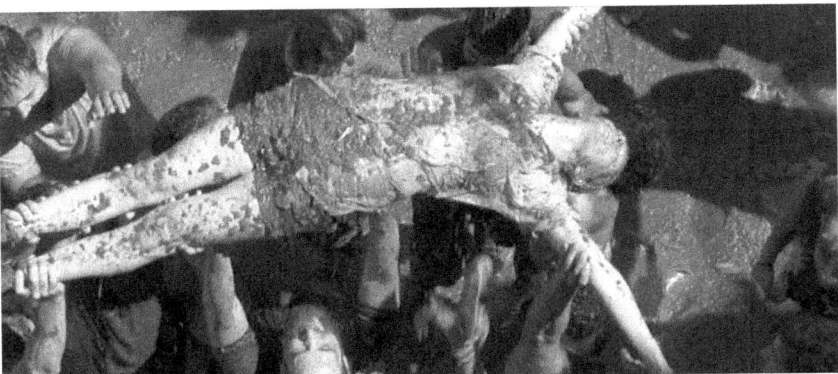

Figure 22 Eva (Tilda Swinton) ecstatic at La Tomatina in *We Need to Talk About Kevin*.

floor of her dwelling, next to her boyfriend's corpse. Where *Morvern Callar* moves from the sensuous to the abject, *We Need to Talk About Kevin* moves from the abject to the sensuous in terms of its visuals, while maintaining its unsettling sound design, recalling Jack Halberstam's discussion of the horror viewer's somatic responses, "a shutter (shudder?)" (1995: 127). In *We Need to Talk About Kevin* the sound design is deliberately used to produce *unexpected* responses in the viewer. The domestic setting is immediately de-stabilized by auditory memories intruding into a mysterious space. The travel narrative of bodily ecstasy is ruptured, in conjunction with the extradiegetic soundtrack that suggests intrusive thoughts or traumatic memories. This deliberate choice in terms of sound mixing and juxtaposed visual elements works to establish an unconventional link between Eva and her murderous son Kevin early on, by suggesting that the rapture Eva experiences at La Tomatina may be akin to whatever Kevin feels when he murders and injures his peers. Eva's memories of her life before becoming a mother, of her time as a solo adventurer, are now inextricable from her imaginings of Kevin's crime. This visual and aural strategy also corresponds to Creed's acknowledgment of the cultural belief that mothers create monstrosities through their imaginations—this early sequence establishes that Eva can only imagine what Kevin feels, but suggests a deep, inarticulate connection between them.[1] Even though *We Need to Talk About*

---

[1] In this sense, the bond between Kevin and Eva is the dark twin to the tender affinity between mother and daughter in Sciamma's *Petite Maman*.

Kevin is not classified as a horror film (nor is *Morvern Callar* for that matter), both films deploy directed listening for the attentive listener and viewer, in order to produce unexpected responses, alongside the display of violence and blood in domestic settings.

Without dialogue, or a dominant musical soundtrack, both of these opening sequences in *We Need to Talk About Kevin* and *Morvern Callar* contain instances of sound design that might go unnoticed by the casual listener/viewer. But, they are both examples of moments that are shaped by Halberstam's click of fear. In *Morvern Callar,* the absence of dialogue at the film's beginning forces us to attend to the subtle noise made by the flashing Christmas tree lights, the quality of the light used to illuminate the bodies on screen, and the small gestures made by Samantha Morton as Morvern, as she shifts her body on the floor. In *We Need to Talk About Kevin* we hear the roar of a crowd and sounds that correspond to the squelch of buckets of liquified tomato pulp coming into contact with flesh, but we sense that something is awry as the crowd sounds shift into a more panicked register, and the thuds of buckets of tomato pulp take on a metallic quality, echoing the way the sound of metal dominates in the later massacre sequence, where Kevin seals the doors to the high school gymnasium with bright yellow bike locks.

Both of these opening sequences also create a texture of quiet that works to privilege the supine bodies of women in unconventional ways. In both *Morvern Callar* and *We Need to Talk About Kevin*, the supine bodies of the protagonists appear but not in the sense that we are used to seeing them in classical art. In *The Reclining Nude*, Emma Wilson comments on this figure across the work of Agnès Varda, Catherine Breillat, and Nan Goldin. Wilson writes, "Lying prone, I am knocked off my axis; I am more animal, more lavish, more extended. I am in a different, more intimate, more open relation to the viewer who beholds me" (2019: 37). Both Eva and Morvern are more animal and more extended in these sequences. While Eva is depicted as ecstatic in the opening sequence, her bodily experience rests somewhere else, ascribed to neither the realm of the sexual nor the spiritual. She is neither Cleopatra bitten by the asp, nor is she Saint Theresa. Held aloft by other revelers in a crucifixion pose, Eva opens her eyes, momentarily aware of other thoughts, before being lowered into a pool of red. In *Morvern Callar*, the feeling of warm intimacy created by a golden-red light is ruptured almost immediately with a shot of Morvern's hand delicately moving across the wounded wrist of her beloved. Both of these sequences evoke the quotation from Louis-Ferdinand Céline that Julia Kristeva places at the start of her chapter entitled "Suffering and Horror" in *Powers of Horror*: "on est puceau de l'horreur come on est puceau de la Volupté" (1982: 142). The attentive viewer and listener to these films becomes the uninitiated, the virgin to horror, learning to shiver for the first time. Our expectations about the kind of story we might encounter are startled, and unmoored by techniques of sound design, and pervasive near-silence, as well as the more animal portrayal of these supine bodies, bodies that are initially presented in voluptuous poses.

Eva's bodily abandon at La Tomatina fades into a duller red-lit scene—the red light that taints present-day Eva's small bungalow, the result of sunlight shining through the paint used to vandalize her windows. Here, Eva is positioned as a previously carefree woman utterly shattered by what has befallen her. But there is something more to be said for this opening juxtaposition: the dark, pokey house is not where Eva wants to be, but nor does she long for the airy, suburban mansion with its billowing sheer draperies. During sequences of Kevin's trial, we hear Eva tell her lawyer she's always "hated the house," which is why she does not care about losing it. The place Eva would still like to be is entirely elsewhere in terms of both place and time: before children, before the "settling down" this has entailed. La Tomatina represents the fantasy of solo travel, of freedom, of pleasurable bodily abandonment. This is the freedom that Eva has surrendered, and this moment represents what she can perhaps never do again. This is what Eva feels motherhood has taken from her and this admission is so taboo that it cannot be spoken, but only shown to us in visual fragments. There is a sense that Eva cannot even admit this to herself, which is why the opening sequence registers as a dream, a mixture of pleasure and trauma that comes unbidden to Eva's sleeping mind.

The shabby bungalow Eva inhabits contrasts with that airy, open plan, suburban mansion that opens the film, a place that is also marked by the unnerving presence of Celie, an angelic blonde child with an eyepatch. Throughout the film, there are scenes of visual doubling that reinforce the twinned nature of Eva and Kevin. The first scene of visual doubling occurs early in the film: in the sink, Eva and teenage Kevin's faces are momentarily blurred together in the water, and this builds on the sense of connection hinted at in the sound mix at the start of the film, a further sense that Kevin may be an expression of Eva's anger, that they remain connected both emotionally and physically.[2]

As the film progresses, *We Need to Talk About Kevin* depicts a complex set of behaviors and emotions around motherhood. Eva, the free-spirited travel writer, finds herself pregnant. Her partner Franklin is excited and expectant, whereas Eva is predominantly resigned if not downright resistant to the constraints and conventions of motherhood and family life. The resignation with which we see Eva approach pregnancy is similar to her resignation at the repeated prison visits to Kevin as he approaches his eighteenth birthday (and the implied transfer to an adult prison population). Later, Eva quietly endures repeated insults as a notorious, public woman: the mother of a school shooter. Eva spends most of the film silently branded as a bad mother and a bad woman, a woman who has failed to raise a suitable son, who has failed to protect her family, who has also failed to immediately embrace her role as mother. While it is clear that other people are more than ready to name Eva as a bad mother, no one ever uses these words to her, and instead hatred is communicated through gestures: the red paint sprayed onto the white house, and the woman who viciously slaps Eva's face in the parking lot. Even Kevin's hatred toward Eva is largely expressed through behavior; his refusal to toilet train that is portrayed as deliberate and malicious, his listlessness when she tries to engage him in play or conversation at virtually any age, and when he becomes a teenager, he exudes both shamelessness and outright malice when she accidentally opens the door to him masturbating in the bathroom. Figure 23 shows Kevin's disturbing look, which he levels at Eva, while he continues masturbating, unfazed by her interruption.

These combined gestures signal Kevin's malevolence, a malevolence he never tries to conceal from Eva, and which he realizes she is too embarrassed to confront him about, because of the way it implicates her as a "bad" mother. In her examination of bad mothers in horror cinema, Eike Träger notes:

---

[2] Because this *isn't* horror cinema, Eva never gets to growl out her anger the way Nola (Samantha Eggar) does in *The Brood*, with her provocation, "I disgust you!" when she is finally in her final form, spawning numerous angry, demonic offspring from her torso.

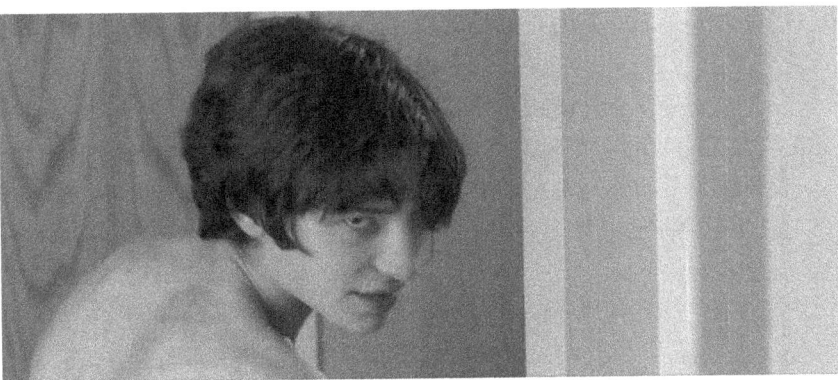

Figure 23 Kevin's (Ezra Miller) malicious sneer when Eva catches him masturbating in *We Need to Talk About Kevin*.

As a genre of excess, the horror mother is often portrayed as either "good in every way" or "bad to the bone." In the former case, she is celebrated as a martyr-like defender of angelic purity, whereas in the latter she is "rightfully" punished for the corruption of an otherwise ideal being from which she fully derives her right to exist. The outrageous violence with which the sons of horror films usually "defy" their evil mothers points towards the "privileged" place that vast parts of society attribute to the mother in the process of psychic individuation, which stems from an assumed closeness of mother and child in the initially dyadic relationship and this closeness in turn 'requires' a particularly forceful separation of the two.

(2017: 2010)

In *We Need to Talk About Kevin*, Eva seems intent on this kind of forceful separation through her loathing of Kevin, while Kevin constantly reinforces their inseparableness by his refusal to be shamed or punished. Ramsay's film pokes at the supposed closeness of the bond between mother and son, by punishing Eva for Kevin's actions and leaving Kevin's imprisonment largely in the background.

In flashback to the early years of her courtship with Franklin, we hear his voice on the phone, pleading "Eva, when are you coming home? I miss you!"—we can hear the longing in his voice, and we see their passionate reunion as they embrace in a rainy street, and then have unprotected sex. We know the sex here is careless, abandoned, frantic, as Franklin asks: "you sure about this?" and this is coupled with the use of microscopic footage of fertilization, indicating that Eva's pregnancy isn't planned. And Eva, of course, pays for this lack of caution. It is Franklin who asks her "is it safe?" and "are you sure?" locating conception as somehow Eva's sole action and decision. This later serves to reinforce her solo responsibility for Kevin's malevolence, and the deaths of Franklin and Celie. From this moment, Eva begins to assume the mantle of bad mother.

Sarah Louise Smyth reads the moment of conception somewhat differently: "In an early scene, Eva makes the conscious decision—or choice—to become pregnant, with the moment of conception marked with Franklin asking, 'are you sure about this?' 'Choice' of course is a critical if contentious word in feminism's vocabulary, particularly in relation to women's reproductive rights" (2020). While I agree with Smyth in terms of how the film configures Eva as responsible for becoming pregnant through Franklin's questions to her in these intimate moments, the tone of the sex we see here, and their ecstatic embraces leading up to it suggest an enthusiastic reunion after a long separation, and the spontaneity and lack of caution that might characterize such an encounter. Franklin's question to Eva suggests that any responsibility for preventing pregnancy has been surrendered to her, and therefore everything that happens from this point onwards may be laid at her door.

With Eva's second (and far more planned) pregnancy, Franklin has failed to notice Eva's changing body until Kevin flatly comments, "Mummer's fat." Franklin is frustrated and asks her:

> Franklin: "When were you gonna tell me?"
> Eva: "Soon ... now"
> Franklin: "How am I part of the decision now? What am I supposed to say now?"

Here, Celia's conception is also configured as Eva's doing. This is a film in which pregnancy and motherhood are a duty and decision placed wholly on Eva. Franklin is entirely peripheral, in spite of the subtle performance on offer from John C. Reilly, who portrays Franklin as a kind, well-meaning partner and caring father who is utterly oblivious to Eva's rage, and to Kevin's sinister qualities. Reilly's portrayal of Franklin also works to support a reading of events that cements Eva's position as bad mother, since it seems that she is the only person who perceives Kevin as malevolent.

Part of the horror and ambivalence of Eva's maternal status comes from the depiction of her pregnancy and labor. Eva's labor and Kevin's hospital birth are shown in fragmented mirror reflections, with a blinding overhead light. The sound design conveys the trauma of this experience as Eva screams in agony, while another woman's voice repeatedly says, "Eva, stop resisting." The command to stop resisting has a sinister edge, as Eva has done nothing but resist a conventional career and domesticity and now finds herself trapped by motherhood. Figure 24 clearly shows the deep difference between Eva and Franklin's experience of becoming a parent.

In many ways this sequence is an evocative visualization of Maggie Nelson's observation in *The Argonauts*: "*You don't do labor*, I was counselled several times before the baby came. *Labor does you*" (2015: 167). Labor and the ensuing experience of caring for an infant have indeed "done" Eva. Kevin's infant screams are constant, grating, and people stare as she wheels the pram along the sidewalk, exhausted and barely upright. Even at this early stage, we see Eva being silently judged by other people as a bad mother, a woman who has failed to be correct in public. Kevin's screams can be heard even over a jackhammer, and Eva seems to experience a moment of relief at the change in sound, grateful for the sound of the city blunting Kevin's wails.

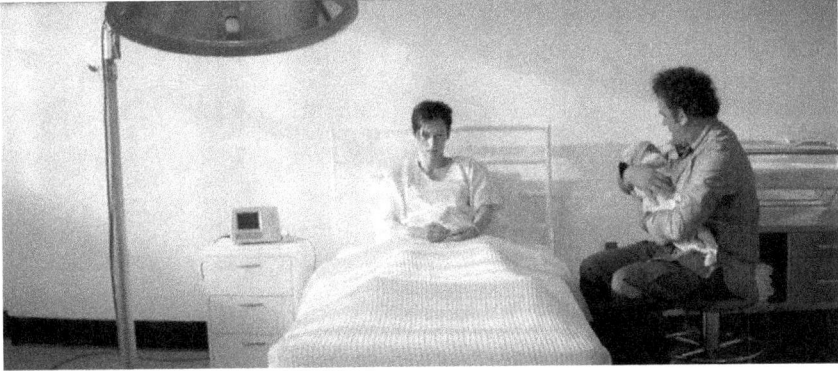

Figure 24 Eva stares coldly ahead while Franklin (John C. Reilly) cradles infant Kevin in *We Need to Talk About Kevin*.

By contrast, Franklin remains oblivious to Eva's suffering and exhaustion during Kevin's infancy. He arrives home from work, and immediately picks up Kevin after Eva insists he's only just fallen asleep, while she is collapsed on the sofa. This establishes a pattern where Kevin consistently alters his behavior for Franklin, appearing happy, grateful, and pleased when he interacts with his father. With Eva, Kevin is silent, belligerent, and increasingly hostile. This escalates in his teens, with his suspected killing of Celia's guinea pig, followed by the loss of Celia's eye in a domestic accident, and then the school shooting.

Nowhere is Eva's discomfort with her first pregnancy more evident than in the sequence depicting the changing room of a prenatal yoga class. Surrounded, by fit, glowing, expectant mothers, Eva clearly does not share in this feeling. Her silence, as she gazes at her own shape, in contrast to the caressing vitality of the other pregnant people once more communicates the unspeakableness of her ambivalence about motherhood.

Eva's feelings are so taboo they can never be voiced, but can only be portrayed through a deeply ambivalent look or stare, as can be seen in Figure 25. Here, she barely even begins to undress, before getting up and exiting the changing room, leaving behind its harp music, and the soft chatter of expectant mothers. As Sue Thornham comments in her reading of the film "as individualised subjects women are urged to mobility and self-definition; as mothers they are re-embodied and returned to place" (2013: 10). Eva's experience of pregnancy

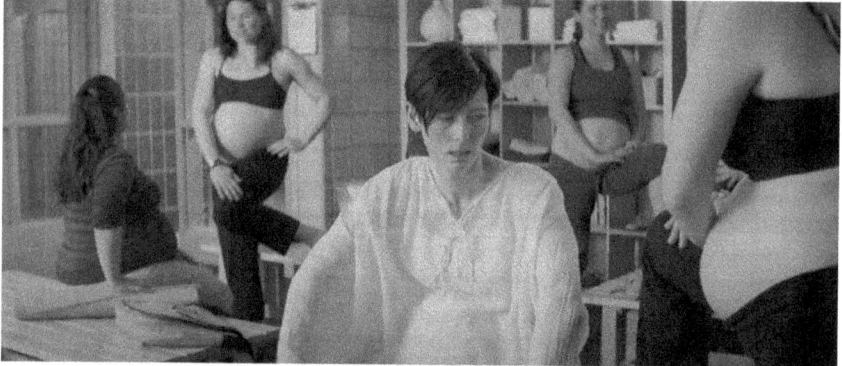

Figure 25 Eva's ambivalence in the pregnancy yoga changing room in *We Need to Talk About Kevin*.

reinforces this view, contrasting it with her previous iteration as globe-trotting travel writer, now living not even in the metropolis, but in a suburban mansion. Eva's clear loathing of the pregnancy yoga changing room and the other mothers is palpable here; it is a place filled with radiant, expectant bodies who seem to be almost shoving their bellies into Eva's face. Coming out of that space, Eva is then overwhelmed in the corridor by a surge of child ballerinas on their way to dance class. Her impassive expression at this sight conveys both indifference and exhaustion; a scene that should be charming is here rendered claustrophobic and oppressive. Eva is hemmed in on all sides: by culture, by her own body, by the corridor walls.

Tilda Swinton's performance as Eva is also important here, as So Mayer remarks, "At every turn, she undermines the conventional role of daughter/wife/mother" (2015). In *We Need to Talk About Kevin*, Swinton as Eva presents as someone who is perhaps much closer to Shelia Heti's examination of not becoming a mother: "I had never dreamed of being a mother. Even as a young girl, it was something I had not wanted to do. I wanted to have boyfriends, and make art, and have interesting conversations and friends" (2018: 129). Heti's description could easily be applied to pre-child Eva (or indeed to Morvern Callar)—these are women who are interested in things besides motherhood. But perhaps Eva is still in thrall to the lure of the mothering instinct, the social pressure of the expectation to have a child, or the idea that one cannot be considered a family unless a household includes children. Heti wonders about the power not just of social pressure but of instinct and bodily feeling itself: "Will you one day feel about the mothering instinct the same way you now feel about the sex instinct, which also suddenly turned on? … you'll resist it, but in retrospect, it took you. You didn't make a choice to go in that direction. Life—nature—pulled your strings" (Heti 104). In nearly every moment of her first pregnancy, Eva seems to still be trying to resist where her body has taken her. Despite her painful, frustrating experience of pregnancy and infant care with Kevin, she opts to become pregnant a second time. When Celia is born, Eva seems to settle into motherhood, experiencing tenderness and joy in her interactions with her daughter. But this does not erase those earlier ambivalent experiences, and instead throws Kevin's malevolence into even sharper focus.

This turn in the narrative problematizes an easy reading of Eva as bad mother, since we witness how differently she behaves with Celie. Kevin's presence in the house, his cruelty, his secrecy, and particularly the way he is seen playing into Franklin's seemingly uncomplicated expectations of fatherhood are particularly disturbing.

The scene where Eva attempts to bond with the teenage Kevin recalls some of Barbara Creed's ideas on motherhood in horror cinema: "what kind of maternal desire, then, does the *The Brood* posit as illegitimate? First, the desire—conscious or otherwise—for woman to give birth without the agency of the male; and second, woman's desire to *express* her desires, specifically her anger" (Creed 1993: 46). In this sequence, Eva and Kevin play mini golf and then go to dinner. Throughout this sequence, as can be seen in Figure 26, the visual similarity between the chic Eva and the handsome, bristling Kevin is palpable as they stand side by side, angry at the limitations of their suburban surroundings.

The silent questions being posed here seem to be "Is Eva a bitch because she and Kevin are too similar?" or "Is Kevin a bitch because they are too similar?" This is reinforced by the performances, as well as the emphasis on physical similarities between Tilda Swinton and Ezra Miller: the decision to present both actors with a similar dark cap of hair, their cold eyes, their cruel sneers, their androgynous swaggers. In this sequence in particular they

Figure 26 Kevin and Eva's visual similarities emphasized in *We Need to Talk About Kevin*.

are too much the same: brittle, nervy, competitive.³ Before they go to dinner, Kevin deliberately consumes part of a roast chicken, which annoys Eva not only because it removes the possibility of eating together, but because it is an assertion of Kevin's power. Throughout the film Kevin's way of eating is depicted as grotesque, disturbing, even abject. In this sequence Eva must eat in the restaurant while Kevin watches her. While she eats and attempts conversation, Kevin destroys a bread roll and verbally eviscerates her attempts at connection, demonstrating the extent to which he sees through his mother, and that he does not see her gesture of connection as sincere. In fact, Kevin spends much of his time in the restaurant offering a description of what Eva would say to him if he were to play along with this charade of togetherness. He snidely comments that she would sensitively attempt to probe him for curiosity about drugs, and that she would tolerantly caution him about practicing safer sex. All the while Eva is silent, appalled, but perhaps also relieved. This mother-son bonding opportunity is so clearly something Eva is attempting because she feels she has to, much in the same way she seems to have carried through with her pregnancy because somewhere deep down, she too cannot escape the idea of the maternal instinct. Her silence in this sequence and on the subject of how she truly feels about being a mother are the gaps that make Kevin into an example of Creed's illegitimate maternal desire. Here, Kevin is the voice of Eva's anger not just at what motherhood has taken from her, but her anger at the ways in which convention now compels her to behave.

Evolution

In *Evolution*, we are initially presented with a seemingly idyllic image of mother and son. The mother cares for the son, preparing food for him, and supervising his play by the rocky shore of the island they inhabit. They

---

[3] There are strong physical similarities between Tilda Swinton and Julie-Marie Parmentier the actor who plays Nicolas's mother in *Evolution*. Parmentier as well as Roxane Duran who plays Stella the nurse who rescues Nicola later in the film are both costumed and made up to be as physically similar as possible. These pale, red-haired, women bear more than a passing resemblance to how Swinton looked in her youth. Eva, Stella, and Nicolas's mother all possess a certain coldness and it is perhaps this quality that makes these images of motherhood so unsettling—they are, in their way, as transgressive as Alice Lowe's pregnant serial killer Ruth in *Prevenge* (2017).

exchange few words, but seem to live a simple, contented life in a small village. But all is not as it seems; in this story both the adult and the child participate in the physical work of birth and motherhood: the nourishing of another body, and the carrying of life. The relationship between boy and woman here is complicated, as it moves beyond that of mother and son. Nicolas will become an experimental host to alien offspring; and later when he befriends Stella the young nurse, their relationship takes on qualities that go well beyond that of caregiver and patient.

Silent, prone bodies appear frequently throughout *Evolution*. We see Nicolas being given medicine at regular intervals—a green liquid diluted in water. Nicolas and the other boys are subject to regular medical check-ups at the local hospital, a dark and sinister place where very little is ever explained. Women tell the boys to do things, but most of what the boys undergo is never spoken about. The nature of the work that goes on at the hospital is hinted at, when we see the women who work there silently watching a video of a caesarean birth.

If the silences that characterize Eva's pregnancy in *We Need to Talk About Kevin* and her relationship with Kevin are troubling, the imagery presented in *Evolution* is even more so. There is an alien physicality depicted in *Evolution* that allows a transgressive, eerie bond between child and caregiver. The clone-like sameness of the adult women contrasts with the individuated boys, and the absence of any children that can be read as female creates a sense of strangeness common to science fiction and horror narratives. Patricia Pisters describes the film's visual approach as taking "the striking formal elements of the same colour palette and abstraction [to] infuse Creed's notions of monstrous motherhood with new elements of ambiguity and ambivalence, addressing the feminine and the female in non-human ways" (2020: 150). In addition to the film's visual register, the film's strange atmosphere is also underscored by its sparse use of dialogue and unsettling, pervasive silence. In combination, the visual uniformity of the women and the lack of dialogue help to present even the most quotidian aspects of motherhood as strange: the preparation of food and the supervising of bathing are rendered bizarre in *Evolution*.

We Need to Talk About Kevin shares something of this approach, consistently depicting Kevin's eating habits as disturbing or revolting, and the suburban house and supermarket as eerily anonymous and muted locations, devoid of individuality. The ways in which these interiors are filmed in *We Need to Talk About Kevin* suggest that Eva clearly perceives these locations as a kind of prison, and every attempt she makes to individualize these spaces either through action or voice is foiled, reinforcing the fact that she cannot escape her role as bad mother. In *Evolution*, Nicolas seems to be attentively mothered at first, but he grows increasingly suspicious of everything that is taking place, sensing that something is not quite right in his world. Once he begins to spend more time in the hospital, and to observe changes to his own body and those of his peers, his suspicions about what these actions of mothering conceal are confirmed. Here, what presents as attentive mothering is more like animal husbandry, or even the careful cultivation of living test subjects who must still be treated in a humane way: groomed, fed, medically surveyed.

Being Unlikeable

At the Q&A following the Edinburgh preview screening of *Prevenge* in January 2017, director, actor, and writer Alice Lowe remarked of Ruth, the film's protagonist whom she played while pregnant: "No one asks if Travis Bickle is likeable." In *King Kong Theory*, Virginie Despentes remarks, "No one feels obliged to write that [Michel] Houellebeq is good-looking. If he were a woman whose books were admired by that many men, they would have written that he was handsome" (2006/2010: 112). These two anecdotes sum up the contradictions embodied in the portrayals of motherhood in *We Need to Talk About Kevin* and *Evolution*. Even though it is Kevin who has committed a massacre, it is Eva who is continually vilified. Nicolas is seemingly both cared for and the subject of medical experiments. Both Eva and Nicolas's unnamed mother enact a selfishness which cannot be articulated verbally, only shown. None of these mothers or caregiving figures are particularly likeable, but these films do not feel the need to justify this. The silence of these films allows unlikeable mothers and caregivers to simply exist, albeit in forms which are still physically beautiful. That said, Tilda Swinton's transformation from elegant and cosmopolitan to haggard and broken is part of *We Need to Talk*

About Kevin's power in portraying the devastation that can be wrought by motherhood. So Mayer describes Swinton as "brandishing her pallor of skin as a butoh-like mask, she draws attention to the persistent conceit that the female performer is simultaneously a blank surface for projection and a doll-puppet smiling at will" (Mayer 2015). As Eva, Swinton is alternately thrilling, unlikeable, and sympathetic. Complaining to Kevin about fat people while they play mini-golf she is cruel and glamorous; later attempting to regain some semblance of pleasure at the travel agency Christmas party, she's insulted by a colleague after she rejects his advances when he whispers "where do you get off? You stuck up bitch." And of course, in the court of public opinion, Eva is a stuck-up bitch. Even after everything that's happened to her, she is not grateful for this man's attention. This, along with the selfishness she displays (a quality that is still regarded as particularly dangerous and repellent in women, and especially mothers), is part of her monstrousness.

In *Evolution*, Nicolas's mother and Stella the nurse who eventually helps Nicolas to escape are presented as either cold, or performing the gestures of caregiving in a sinister way, as if they have been learned by rote. Stella in particular seems to have few physical boundaries when it comes to caring for Nicolas in hospital, even encouraging him to shower with her, which he refuses to do so alone. In order to escape the hospital, Stella must share her underwater breathing capacity with Nicolas, confirming that there is indeed something sea-creaturely about Stella and the other women.

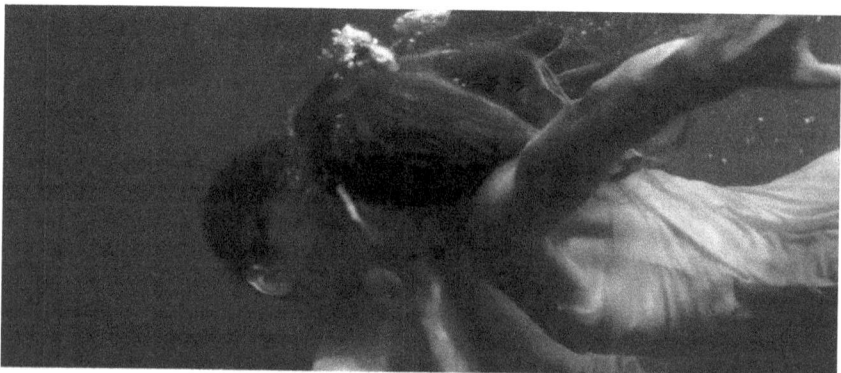

Figure 27 Stella (Roxane Duran) helps Nicolas to breathe underwater in *Evolution*.

Stella's action can be seen in Figure 27 and this registers as a physical intimacy that is not entirely appropriate; while it is not exactly a sexual gesture, she and Nicolas are joined at the mouth in what resembles a kiss. Mary Russo notes that "the grotesque body is the open, protruding, extended, secreting body, the body of becoming, process and change" (Russo 1994: 62–3). This description might be easily applied to the strange and unsettling gesture between Stella and Nicolas, as Stella's breathing capacity extends out toward Nicolas, and the way Nicolas's body becomes grotesque through medical interventions to which he cannot consent. We can also link this to how the bodies of the boys in *Evolution* are perceived by their mothers. They are given medication for their changing bodies, bodies that will soon be subject to surgical intervention. Although neither Nicolas nor his mother appears physically unusual at first, he soon discovers all is not as it seems with regards to his mother's body, as Pisters notes: "When he later sees his mother taking a shower, he notices strange suction cups on her back, revealing her squid-like, cephalopod nature" (Pisters 2020: 151). This cephalopodness is reinforced by the ink-like tincture Nicolas is given as medicine, and the strange ritual where he observes the women gathering at night on the beach, and then writhing naked in the sand.

Monstrous Vessels

Coldness and selfishness, coupled with the presentation of the maternal body as grotesque, make these films and their images of motherhood transgressive. In *Evolution*, Nicolas is operated on without his consent, his body is made into a maternal vessel for two monstrous, alien infants who we see only briefly, still attached to him in a tank of murky, slimy water. In terms of abjection, the use of this tank as a kind of bathtub, an object normally used to rid the body of dirt, is here used as the place to nourish new life amongst dirt and filth. In *Powers of Horror*, Kristeva remarks "the fact remains that all food is liable to defile" (Kristeva 1982: 75) and food as an aspect of abjection features substantially in both *We Need to Talk About Kevin* and *Evolution*. In *Evolution*, Nicolas is given food that is an abjectification of a beloved childhood staple: slimy, green, and worm-like; it resembles nothing so much as an inversion of pasta noodles. This is the only food we ever see Nicolas consume, and therefore the connection to the abject is established early and silently, as Nicolas's bodily boundaries are transgressed by food that appears disgusting, just as his body is probed by doctors in ways he does not understand. This serves to establish something of the film's unsettling tone, destabilizing otherwise ordinary domestic scenes of what appear, at first glance, to be a mother preparing food for her child. This is precisely the kind of linkage described by Kristeva: "Food becomes abject only if it is a border between two distinct entities or territories. A boundary between nature and culture, between the human and the non-human" (75). In *Evolution*, this unpalatable looking food establishes the transgression of conventions surrounding maternity and caregiving, hinting at the film's later revelation of the women's alien bodies, and the careful performance of maternity as a disguise for medical experimentation. In *Evolution*, both motherhood and childhood become abject experiences. Nicolas's body becomes abjectified food for the alien beings he did not even know he was carrying, when we see the infants still attached to his torso in the dirty water tank. While this scene furthers the idea that caregiving and maternity may be performed by anyone, the fact remains that this is essentially a depiction of forced pregnancy. Much like the silence that we find in Sciamma's films that feature child protagonists, this film also uses silence as a field of development for the child gaze. Nicolas uncovers unsettling truths in silence, and he has no one to tell who might rescue him. He also has no language to articulate what is happening to him or his friends, much like the girls of *Innocence*, who can only do as they are instructed. Stella helps him to escape, but quickly abandons him alone in a small boat, as he drifts toward a refinery site where the film ends.

We Need to Talk About Kevin also deals in food as a symbol of abjection. Kevin renders food that would otherwise be palatable to many (a soft white bread roll, a roast chicken, a jam sandwich, a fresh lychee) as something that becomes abject when it comes into contact with his body. Kevin is seen messily devouring the chicken before his dinner with Eva, the sound of slurping, chewing, and jellied fat permeates this scene, and Kevin has not even dismembered the chicken; he has simply ripped into it with his teeth, holding it with both hands.

In the restaurant he refuses food, instead destroying the bread roll without eating it, rolling the soft inner flesh into little balls as he reveals his open contempt for Eva's parenting. Perhaps the most disturbing moment is when Kevin eats a fresh lychee; all while his parents try to discuss his role in the serious eye injury sustained by his younger sister Celia; the lychee's clear resemblance to an eyeball is queasy and unmistakable, as he sinks his teeth into the soft flesh of the fruit, this further emphasizes Kevin's callousness. In this sequence, Kevin reaches for the lychee as the topic of Celia's injury is broached. He begins peeling the fruit, and he seems relaxed and nonchalant, not in the least uncomfortable. We see a close-up of his fingers digging into the lychee's tough outer skin in order to reveal its soft inside. Peeled, he places the fruit in his mouth, causing juice to spurt out as he replies to his mother's remark "I thought you didn't like those" with "Oh they're … what would you call it? An acquired taste." Franklin remains calm and impassive but Eva angrily gets up from the table, having correctly interpreted this display as yet more evidence of Kevin's lack of compassion. As he grows older, Kevin is portrayed as the vessel for his mother's sublimated anger and his own aggression begins to display itself in relation to the food he consumes, his sister's body, family pets, and eventually results in his killing of both Franklin and Celia, as well as a number of his peers.

Anger and Unlikeability

Eva has clearly been subject to more than just public notoriety during Kevin's trial—she too has become a figure of blame, despite the deaths of Celia and Franklin at Kevin's hands. She has not been able to move away from the area where the killings occurred, and therefore she regularly encounters other women who despise her; she is slapped in the street, her packet of eggs is smashed in the supermarket, her house vandalized, and her neighbors shun her. All of these instances reinforce Eva's status as not just an unlikeable character, but a mother who has been publicly vilified for her unlikeableness. Sheli Heti writes that "the woman who doesn't have a child is looked at with the same aversion and reproach as a grown man who doesn't have a job. Like she has something to apologize for. Like she's not entitled to pride" (Heti 270). Here, Eva may as well be a woman without a child, even though Kevin is still alive in prison. Her community repeatedly reminds her that she is not entitled to exist, and yet she persists. The later revelation that Eva maintains a bedroom for Kevin, keeping it pristine and austere just as he left it, further cements their deep connection, one that is not easy to shuck off. The seemingly ordinary, domestic tasks of painting walls and making a bed instead become something else. These gestures ask us to consider whether Eva continues to visit Kevin, and to keep a bedroom for him because, now that he has committed an atrocity, he has done what she cannot. This renders Eva, in the end, similarly monstrous to the mothers-who-are-not of *Evolution*. She too performs acts of care almost by rote, for a son that she has never cherished until he commits a crime so terrible that he is likely to remain in prison for most of his adult life. Kevin's bedroom is not the eerily maintained bedroom of a murdered teenage girl, but it is a kind of shrine. It is the space Eva has finally made for Kevin, the avatar of her silent, bristling anger, anger at everything she has been unable to do since becoming a mother. In this light, the hostility directed at Eva by strangers becomes the result of how some have sensed her desire to burn down everything, to reject motherhood and suburban living, but that she could not bring herself to do this, as if they have seen into her traumatized dream that begins the film, where she fantasizes about her previous life, but knows that the reality of what she has done and in turn what Kevin has done has altered her existence forever.

Other Mothers

In Céline Sciamma's *Tomboy*, Laure/Mikäel is a child who is ultimately bound by the parameters set up by their parents. Initially, Laure/Mikäel seems to be able to exist in a space that becomes increasingly "boyed" (to borrow a phrase from Sara Ahmed). Katharina Lindner notes:

> *Tomboy* traces Laure's negotiation of the different ways in which her embodied experience takes shape and makes sense in the interior and exterior worlds of the film. Gradually, these worlds encroach upon each

other and ultimately, and not surprisingly, they collide. This collision is instigated by the figure of the mother, who comes to stand, and not entirely unproblematically, for the larger social and institutional contexts in which Laure's queer embodiment is not a viable, and intelligible option.

(Lindner 219)

In the concluding moments of *Tomboy*, Laure/Mikael's mother reminds them that school is starting soon, explicitly invoking one of the "institutional contexts" that Lindner says creates a problem for this child's queer embodiment. The mother here wishes things to be defined and transparent. While she is happy to see her child dressing as they like, and choosing the color for their room, she cannot yet conceptualize that her child's gender may differ from the one they have been assigned at birth. The mother in *Tomboy*, from what we learn of her, shares a good deal with the seemingly happy, pretty, idealized mothers Eva can't wait to get away from in the pregnancy yoga changing room. Laure/Mikael's mother is warmer than the mothers-who-are-not of *Evolution*, and her radiant, expectant body alongside the tenderness of her children and partner set her apart from these more sinister images of motherhood.

In *The Souvenir Part I* and *II*, we once more see Tilda Swinton playing a mother, this time opposite her real-life daughter Honor Swinton-Byrne as Julie. At times the performance Swinton delivers as Julie's mother in *The Souvenir Part I* is almost comedic; she plays a certain kind of posh woman who lives happily in the country with her husband and dogs, who cooks and knits, and helps her daughter furnish the flat they have helped her to buy. In *The Souvenir Part II*, we see more of this character as Julie retreats to her childhood home to grieve Anthony's (Tom Burke) death. Julie's mother tends to her, but Julie must push her mother to reveal her own feelings about Anthony, and about Julie's work at film school. This mother and daughter clearly have a close and tender relationship, though in terms of what they say to each other it rarely seems to go beyond surface pleasantries. It is only when Julie accidentally breaks the sugar bowl her mother has made in a pottery course that she realizes how easy it is to hurt her, and how much her mother conceals. In another exchange, Julie admonishes her mother for continuing to smoke, and when asked what her father thinks of this, her mother replies "he pretends he doesn't know anything about it" and claims this is "the sign of a truly loving person." His silence and deliberate inattention to her smoking are considered a sign that he truly loves her, and does not desire to change her behavior. This kind of silence may well be the province of a particular kind of upper-class marriage, where a couple stays together partly by deliberately overlooking the things that would otherwise cause the relationship to dissolve. And yet, Julie's mother signals this silence as something she values, as a sign of being able to tolerate the faults of the person you love.

This loving silence is something that Hogg wrestles with in her earlier films, particularly in the relationships we witness in *Unrelated* and *Archipelago*. In *Unrelated*, Oakley (Tom Hiddleston) has a troubled, aggressive relationship with his father and his mother is absent. Verena (Mary Rosco) acts as a capable, organized, and highly compassionate image of motherhood in midlife, whose children are now teenagers nearing adulthood. She is also someone with the capacity to offer some of her maternal grace to Anna, and it is no surprise that it is Verena who holds and comforts Anna when she confesses her grief at embarking on menopause.

Somewhere between Eva the bad mother, and the mysterious, alien, mothers-who-are not of *Evolution* lie these other images of motherhood, of women who have found contentment in this role (as we see in *Unrelated*, *Archipelago*, and *The Souvenir Part I* and *II*) but who are, for the most part, not the protagonists of those stories. Even Laure/Mikäel's mother is not the protagonist of *Tomboy*, and she occupies a space that does little to detract from the ideals of motherhood, and even her actions toward her eldest child may change as she comes to understand them further. None of these other mothers are monstrous, or controlling, but they do not seem ambivalent either. Ambivalence is something that belongs to the artist/exhibitionst, or those women of a certain age who have chosen not to become mothers.

The question of whether or not *We Need to Talk About Kevin* and *Evolution* are horror films is tricky. I used to be convinced they weren't and now I'm far less sure. *Evolution* is easier to place in this category, with its deep unease about bodies and care-taking roles. *We Need to Talk About Kevin* sits less easily as a horror, though it too trades in unease and taboo. If the baseline for horror is whether or not it makes you afraid, then both of these films do that—it asks us what might happen if we acknowledge that not all women want to be mothers.

5

Silenced Desire and Anger in Joanna Hogg's *Unrelated*, *Archipelago*, and *Exhibition*

Nearly a decade ago, Sharon Hinchliff issued the following call to arms "When it comes to women, ageing and sexuality, a plurality of stories is required" (2014: 75). These three films all take up Hinchliff's challenge by featuring middle-aged women past forty and their struggles with desire, anger, and creativity. Joanna Walsh's observation that "a successful marriage dissolves into silence" (2018: 90) applies to some of the relationships on display here: between Anna and Patricia and their unseen partners in *Unrelated*, and *Archipelago*, and between D and H in *Exhibition*. Silence becomes an integral part of these characters' struggles, whether they are individual or interpersonal and silence is often the canvas onto which these themes and problems are mapped. This silence takes several forms: the unvoiced feeling concealed by small talk, the quiet intensity of solo working, and the illicit affinity. These forms recall Vogelin's ideas of silence as a radical space for knowing the self, and therefore the silence that occurs in these films takes the form of absences, and the expression of emotions or affinities that are never fully articulated verbally but may be represented in other ways, through bodily gestures and looks.

As Ciara Barrett notes, "Hogg's films have prominently featured middle-aged female protagonists, a demographic still afforded relatively scant narrative attention in either mainstream or independent cinema" (2015: 1).[1] *Unrelated* offers us Anna (Kathryn Worth), an attractive woman in her late forties who engages in a flirtation with a younger man, Oakley (Tom Hiddleston), during a

---

[1] Serial television has a stronger record in affording middle-aged female protagonists narratives, particularly in the crime and legal drama genres. Women over forty also feature prominently in pornography, particularly under the "MILF" tag. While this is a popular and lucrative category, an open erotic appreciation of older women remains somewhat taboo at least in heterosexual scenarios.

group holiday in Tuscany which includes her friends who are parents and their late teen and adult children. Toward the end of the film, Anna reveals to her friend Verena that she is now menopausal and will never have children with her partner (with whom she has been fighting and who never appears in the film, not unlike Patricia's absent husband in *Archipelago*). Yet, Anna is never portrayed as tragic or clichéd. She is not desperate to prove her desirability to anyone, nor does she seem concerned about her child-free status until the end of the film, when she mourns the closing off of this part of her life. Instead, the film has much in common with Ramsay's *Morvern Callar*, where travel serves as a path to self-reflection and actualization.

Unrelated and *Exhibition* both feature protagonists who are middle-aged, conventionally attractive, and physically active (Anna runs daily, D swims and practices yoga). Anna and D are hardly the most overt examples of what has been termed "new ageing"[2] where looking younger than one's age is equivalent with looking attractive, but this does play a part in their narrative trajectory, particularly in *Unrelated*, where Anna must come to terms with the reality of the end of fertility. The silences that punctuate *Unrelated* tend to underscore Anna's self-evaluation, as she watches how the various family dynamics play out around her. Many scenes in *Unrelated* are filled with chatter, but this feels like aural wallpaper, drawing attention to the way we often fill up what might be uncomfortable silence. Moments of genuine quiet (when conversation is not always at a discernible level) signal contemplation, or draw attention to Anna's loneliness, particularly when her presence becomes a divisive force, after she reveals she has been present during a car accident with Oakley and the other young people, and after Oakley has rejected her sexual invitation. In *Exhibition*, D's silence has two distinct forms: the busy, thinking silence of artistic practice as she tries out textures, and postures for her performances, as well as a deeply restful silence accompanying sequences where she is swimming or doing yoga alone. Where Anna is isolated without wishing to be, and unsure of whether she ought to disclose anything about her menopause

---

[2] Sarah Falcus and Katsura Sako discuss this idea in their chapter "Women, Travelling and Later Life" in *Ageing, Popular Culture and Contemporary Feminism: Harleys and Hormones*. Edited by Imelda Whelehan and Joel Gwynne (2014).

or her relationship difficulties, D chooses to spend a great deal of time alone and silent.

In *Archipelago* and *Exhibition*, setting is important in terms of silence and the absence of dialogue. *Archipelago*, set on the Scilly Isles, makes use of the sound of the landscape in outdoor scenes which impinges on too much dialogue, and characters concentrate in silence as they work on creating watercolor paintings in situ. In *Exhibition*, the quietude of the house inhabited by D and H, and their need to maintain separate workspaces within it, the negotiation of when interruption is desired or acceptable, creates a space of deep quiet that signals a perfect crucible for making art.

In contrast to the other two films, Patricia (Kate Fahy), the mother in *Archipelago*, is somewhat marginalized in comparison to Anna and D. Patricia is not the "silent elderly women who haunt the frame" in *Innocence* (Mroz 290). However, she is unusual in Hogg's oeuvre as the only one of her protagonists who has children, though both are adults. Like Anna and D Patricia has quite a serious occupation: while she is not a professional artist, she is portrayed as investing a great deal of time in making and discussing painting with her tutor, (the real-life artist, Christopher Baker) during the island holiday. Patricia is similar to Verena in *Unrelated*, a woman who is clearly fulfilled and occupied by family life—Verena has organized the entire holiday in Tuscany, she feels obligated to help resolve tensions that arise in the group, and it is she who prods Anna out of silence, to confide in her. Verena has seemingly succeeded in enacting a rather idealized and well-managed version of family life, though there are still arguments and disagreements over which she has no control. In contrast, Patricia has not quite let go of a romantic notion of family life, and in *Archipelago* her attempt to organize the island holiday shows the ways in which her children and husband have moved away from her (crucially, we only hear Patricia's side of the phone conversations she has with her husband). In this sense, Patricia's marginalization, her silence on certain topics, is important as it displays the ways in which she is forgotten and under-appreciated. In contrast, Verena acts as a lively, energetic presence throughout *Unrelated*, providing care, advice, and support to nearly all the other characters at one point or another; yet she is a well-defined character and is portrayed as someone deeply satisfied by her relationships. Hogg's work suggests a variety of ways of representing aging women and their relationships to maternity, in distinct contrast to the troubling, violent images of maternity in the work of Ramsay and Hadžhalilović.

Anna

Unrelated is set during a group holiday in Tuscany, where Anna has been invited to join her old school friend Verena and her new husband Charlie (Michael Hadley). The party also includes several teenagers: Charlie's son Archie (Harry Kershaw), Verena's children Jack (Henry Lloyd Hughes) and Badge (Emma Hiddleston), and her cousin George (David Rintoul) and his adult son Oakley. Rather than socializing predominantly with her own age group, Anna arrives alone and drifts into socializing with the younger people. Early on, Jack relates a mischievous story that involves frolicking in a deserted square, public urination, and being chased by the caribinieri. After the story is finished, Oakley says to Anna "just don't tell the olds, yeah?" and she replies "no, of course I won't." The allure of this designation that Anna is seen as part of the younger group is too much to resist. As a childless, energetic woman who isn't visibly responsible to anyone except herself, she fits more easily with the carefree activities of the younger group.

Unrelated subtly explores what it means to be a participant in an unexpected flirtation. While Oakley is revealed as a selfish, and somewhat arrogant figure toward the end of the film, his attentions to Anna are nonetheless a source of pleasure to her. At dinner on Anna's first full night at the villa, Oakley offers her a cigarette. This classic gesture of potential intimacy is interrupted by Verena who relates "a very good story about Anna and smoking." When they were all at school together, Anna coughed so loudly that she got everyone into trouble for smoking behind the bike sheds. Even though Verena relates this story in a good-natured way, Anna says nothing and smiles quietly at this story which must be from more than twenty-five years ago. She tolerates this gentle mocking by an old friend, even though it attempts to place Anna in a category that suggests she is no fun. Oakley observes Anna while the story is being told (see Figure 32), this story that ought to emphasize the gulf in age, experience, and attitude that exists between them. The story is meant to erect a barrier, but seems to have the opposite effect. Instead of creating a boundary, Oakley seems even more interested in and by Anna; he seems to sense that Anna is someone open to experience, on whom he can try out his charms, and from whom he can gain insight about the pitfalls of long-term relationships.

This sequence at the dinner table initiates a companionable silence between Anna and Oakley, a silence that we might now begin to call flirtatious. At breakfast the following morning Anna lets out her long hair, which she has kept tied up until this moment. When Oakley enters the kitchen, he begins to put himself into Anna's intimate space, wordlessly standing behind her for what feels like a fraction too long and reaching across her, to gauge her reaction to his proximity. Here, Anna does not look directly at Oakley, but her behavior and her gestures suggest she is certainly aware of him, since she does not shy away or attempt to create more space between them. Oakley's look at her is open, receptive, and direct, as if he is waiting for her to meet his gaze and remove all doubt about this affinity that is growing between them. These gestures, combined with the absence of dialogue and a series of shared, often sidelong glances, indicate a space of possibility, and this space is presented as physical gaps between their bodies, but we can also listen for the aural space of their shared silences. These gaps (physical and aural) are more than the difference in age and experience between these characters—in these spaces we see and hear everything that cannot yet be acknowledged or verbally articulated. Anna is conscious of Oakley's presence as he sits next to her, while the others chat away, oblivious. What's important here is the silence that these two characters are sharing, and the fact that no one else seems to notice this. It might suggest that it does not occur to anyone else that these two might share something, and therefore there is nothing to see here, just as there is nothing to hear. But, for the attentive viewer/listener this is a vital moment. Just as Eva's anger and ambivalence in *We Need to Talk About Kevin* cannot be voiced, only shown, we witness a similar taboo with regard to the growing attraction between Anna and Oakley. What is ultimately established in this scene is the beginning of a sense of affinity between these two characters. Both Oakley and Anna are ready to undertake a mutually desiring exchange, but they are waiting for the other person to present an opening. This narrowing of the margins of their personal space signals their mutual interest without recourse to words, or even a gaze being fully met. And of course, this is how flirtation works: it is a feeling simultaneously located in the body, while also creating a distraction from the reality of the body. It lets us put some distance between confronting the truth of physicality, all the body's flaws and failings, as well as its perfections. In his article *Being Cruised*, Jonathan Alexander remarks:

> The drama, such as it is, occurs almost entirely in these varied invitations to look and the exchanges of looks that generate tension because they are not being interpreted or clarified through verbal articulation … Just looking opens up a world of possibility. Looking is all potential.
>
> (2018)

While Alexander is reflecting on his personal experience of navigating the codes of cruising exchanged between queer men, the importance he places on the exchange of looks and what they may contain resonates with this sequence in Hogg's film. Leaving aside for a moment the focus that film studies has historically placed on the look and the gaze when it objectifies the body, what might we make of these lowered, fleeting glances between Anna and Oakley? Recalling Lisa Johnson's idea that *Morvern Callar* deploys a lowered, "shamed gaze [that] seems itself to produce new interest" (1368) we might reflect on whether the silence of this sequence, coupled with the gestures deployed by Worth and Hiddleston, here suggest something of this "new interest," where "looking is all potential." Johnson's idea of a shamed gaze also fits with the taboo nature of the desire between these characters, where the age gap and the stigma of the expression of desire as something inappropriate to older women persist in making this relationship impossible to depict.

On an excursion into Siena, Anna and Oakley sit next to one another in the sloped central square, having the kind of discussion you sometimes have with people who like to overshare in order to establish intimacy. They discuss Italian women, how they are all so beautiful, and Oakley declares, "I just think men and women are always bound to be unfaithful." It's unclear whether this is simply an observation, a deliberate invitation for Anna to be unfaithful to Alex, or a confession from Oakley that he has trouble with monogamy. Anna replies "you're probably right" but counters this with the idea that long-term relationships and specifically marriage are about creating a bond, a life, "not just mere sexual fidelity." Oakley then cuts straight to the heart of the matter, asking Anna if that's what she's working on with her husband, and she dodges this, commenting vaguely, "I can't see that far ahead." They both then comment on Charlie and Verena's marriage, how they seem happy (Verena has called Anna her oldest friend and has already reproached her for not seeming to want to spend time with her, Charlie, and George), though they have only been together for about six years. Oakley returns to the subject of sex and more implicitly, erotic attraction, observing that "if the sex isn't there, you're dead in the water" and then asks Anna "was it ever good?" It's unclear whether this question is about the overall quality of Anna's relationship, a test of the boundaries of their burgeoning connection, or whether Oakley is simply trying out his charms, to see how far they will get him. In the end, it is perhaps a mixture of all of these things, since Anna and Oakley present one another with their shared gazes, and a similar desire to be perceived. Anna declares that desire changes after twelve years together, that "long term relationships are not easy." Oakley then asks her about children, a topic Anna clearly doesn't want to discuss and he apologizes almost immediately. Having touched the edge of a silence that Anna is not ready to broach, Oakley retreats.

Here, Hogg places another taboo subject at the heart of her film, a subject that is also characterized by silence. The question of whether or not one is planning for or wants children is significant; it's something people still ask, but increasingly the attitude toward the acceptability of the question "any kids?" particularly when leveled at women, is being queried. Like some expressions of sexual desire, discussions around the ambivalencies of fertility and pregnancy remain rare. Where Ramsay shows us the monstrous figure of Eva, a woman who regrets her first pregnancy in *We Need to Talk About Kevin*, Hogg shows us Anna who hasn't yet come to terms with her feelings on this subject. Both Anna and Eva use silence to deflect and conceal their taboo feelings of anger or anguish.

On a subsequent evening, after a drunken outing to Siena for a local celebration, Anna and Oakley have been dancing and flirting with increasing intensity. In the summer heat and press of crowds, Oakley has removed his shirt, and on the return journey there is a fleeting shot of the two of them on the descending metro escalator, where Anna embraces him from behind and he lets her do this. Back at the villa, they stand outside the entrance to her room and Anna issues a definitive invitation: "Oakley, you can come in if you want."

Here, Anna is sure of her desire for him. Without hesitation he replies, "I better not" and kisses her cheek. His response is polite, even charming, and he does it without missing a beat. But we can see that Anna reads it for what it is—a clear "no, I'm not going to have sex with you tonight." Oakley's lack of hesitation is devastating and the pain of that rejection is something rarely depicted on screen. Julia Hallam, writing about middle years and older female protagonists, notes that many screen narratives "punish women for expressing desire, emphasising their 'outsider' status within a heteronormative framework of 'respectable' aging femininity" (2016: 553). Certainly, the desires of mature women in mainstream narrative cinema often get treated as a pathology or the butt of jokes. Consider the way that women's desire is treated in films as wildly divergent as *The Seven Year Itch* (Billy Wilder, 1955) and *American Pie* (Paul Weitz, 1999). Women can't keep their hands off men, but this is seen as the source of comedy. In *The Seven Year Itch*, a man fantasizes about nobly resisting the numerous women who throw themselves at him. In *American Pie*, Jennifer Coolidge is the original MILF, the subject of male teen fantasy, but also an object of desire that cannot be viewed with sincerity.[3] Hogg is one of the few filmmakers who consistently explores and represents women at a variety of ages as desirable in her work.

Who Pretty Is For

One of the most interesting examples of Hogg's exploration of mature female desire in *Unrelated* is when Anna shops for lingerie. In the shop, she chooses a black lace bra, and the assistant offers her a range of additional choices: a merry widow corset or thong underwear. Anna declines these items in favor of a matching black lace panty; pretty, but also practical to wear in the

---

[3] Coolidge's career has since built on and transcended this performance, particularly with regard to the critical acclaim she has received for her role in the television series *The White Lotus*.

course of ordinary life. I use the term pretty here deliberately, and in line with how Rosalind Galt defines it in her book *Pretty: Film and the Decorative Image*:

> If pretty is usually rejected as too feminine, too effeminate, and too foreign, it can surely provide aesthetico-political friction for queer or feminist film … *pretty* so immediately brings to mind a negative, even repugnant, version of aesthetic value for many listeners. Feminists hear in the term its diminutive implications: a pretty girl is one who accedes to patriarchal standards of behaviour and self-presentation. Marxists think of prettiness as a quality of the commodity fetish, a central function of ideology's ability to veil real relations. Many critics hear in the term a silent 'merely' in which the merely pretty is understood as a pleasing surface for an unsophisticated audience, lacking in depth, seriousness or complexity of meaning.
>
> (Galt 2011: 6)

Here, the selection of pretty lingerie by a middle-aged woman suggests an enticing knowledge of the self and the body. While this is a transaction that takes place in a shop, Anna's solo journey for seeking these items evokes the image of the flâneuse, and the artist-exhibitionist: a woman who is financially and emotionally independent, and willing to view herself as attractive, in spite of what culture may tell her about what pretty means (youth) and who it is for (patriarchy). While there is the sense that she may be buying these items because she can imagine being seen as desirable by Oakley, there is also a sense that she is still considering what she would like her own body to look like, for herself. Anna buys these items thinking about how she will feel good in them. This too suggests a more deliberate engagement with the body as a more than decorative surface on screen, more than an objectified body. Here, we have pretty in its more radical incarnation, via Cixous's woman's body with its thousand and one plateaus of ardor: adornment and admiration of one's own form is surely one of these. Rather than being "merely" pretty or "merely" vanity, we can consider the presentation of Anna's purchasing decisions, alongside the significance of the sequence in the swimming pool, as a visual expression of her bodily pleasures and desires.

In this earlier pool sequence, Anna has been drinking and dancing with the young people in the wine cellar after dinner, and they all run outside and jump in the pool, where they're joined by Verena and Charlie, who have been lying on the sunloungers in the dark. Oakley, Jack, and Archie all jump in the pool naked, as does Anna, perhaps not realizing that all the other women have elected to at least keep on their underwear. Anna is naked in the water, and the three young men joke with one another about the tension of the moment, making references to shared films from their youth, and the stamina required to be the last one in the pool. Anna laughs a little, but then says she's getting cold and swims to the side of the pool, before pushing herself onto the patio. There is a brief shot of Anna's bottom and toned legs. The young men are visibly struck momentarily silent. In Figure 28, we can make out their serious expressions and stares.

Coming after the initial jokes, the silences in this sequence leave us to consider what it might mean if we just acknowledge that Anna is sexy. The young men all wait and watch her as she climbs out, Archie remarking of the older two "what're you two looking!," while Anna calmly wraps herself in a towel and says "see you in a minute." After she enters the house Archie declares "you guys are such perverts," dispelling the quiet and suggesting blatant voyeurism, but even this is met with silence from Oakley and Jack, whose unwavering attention in the image below suggests a sincere, desiring interest

Figure 28 Archie (Harry Kershaw), Oakley (Tom Hiddleston), and Jack (Henry Lloyd Hughes) stare at Anna in the pool in *Unrelated*.

in Anna's body.[4] Their silence and serious expressions do not suggest disgust or amusement or leering threat. They may well have been taken by surprise at how the sight of Anna has made them feel, as Amia Srinivasan reminds us, "Desire can cut against what politics has chosen for us, and choose for itself" (2022: 91). Here, silence becomes the open field for desire to flourish. Anna does not feign any modesty and the young men continue to look at her. She treats this moment casually, destigmatizing the idea of her naked body as something she ought to be embarrassed about when in fact she isn't embarrassed at all. What feels off-kilter here is how Anna, in her enthusiasm for the late night swim, has failed to conform; where the other women have elected to be less than fully nude, Anna has inadvertently revealed her self-confidence and bodily acceptance. This is confirmed when Anna returns to her room and gazes at her naked reflection before going into the shower. This is not a conventionally eroticized moment, and Hogg shoots Anna from the side, so we can't see what Anna sees in the mirror, but we do see a side view of Anna's lean, tanned body. Calm, quiet, and very relaxed, she strolls into her en-suite bathroom, indicating a satisfaction and a confidence that is extremely rare for women of any age on screen.

It is essential to re-evaluate these moments in *Unrelated*, particularly if we see them in a continuum with the rich and sensuous solo sexuality practiced by D (Viv Albertine) in *Exhibition*, whose fantasies are self-documented, who uses dress for her own pleasure, and whose reveling in her own flesh and movement forms a key component of her art practice, her sexuality, and her everyday life. In *Unrelated*, Hogg hasn't quite got to that place yet. But in *Exhibition* this representation of a mature woman's sexuality as something that is worth taking seriously is in full flower. To acknowledge the pleasures of dress and the body and how it intersects with desire is rather marvelous and, I think, not easy to do. Here, silence becomes a space where the desirable, older feminine body is permitted to exist, to be seen. The casual intimacy of the nudity in the night swim sequence alongside the purchasing of black lingerie all act as silent markers of desire in *Unrelated*.

---

[4] In an interview on the DVD of *Unrelated*, Hogg comments that some audiences have noted a sense of menace in this sequence, but in my view this isn't borne out by the interpersonal relationships that develop throughout the film.

The use of and display of lingerie as a component of sexual practice also takes place in *Exhibition*, where D wears lace underwear and heeled sandals for herself, in order to conduct a solo masturbation fantasy. These instances, alongside the sequence where Anna chooses her black lace lingerie in *Unrelated* (though we don't see her wearing it), speak to the idea of lingerie as a way of showing knowledge of one's own body. In Figure 29, we can see Anna's delight as she chooses items in the shop in Siena. In *Exhibition*, D also wears lace underwear (see Figure 30) as part of her art performance practice, suggesting that there is a costume aspect of lingerie that she is prepared to play with as an artist, and that it is something that can be taken beyond the private realm of the bedroom.

In both *Unrelated* and *Exhibition*, there is no explicit diegetic audience for these instances of the display of lingerie. Even though H watches D through the window as she rehearses a finalized version of her performance toward the end of the film, the underwear is not *for* him, in the sense that the underwear Anthony presents to Julie in *The Souvenir Part I* may be seen as being *for* him (see Figure 31).

Tsaousi and Brewis note that "lingerie in particular is so saturated with erotic cultural connotations that simply putting it on—whether others see it or

Figure 29 Anna (Kathryn Worth) purchasing black lace lingerie in *Unrelated*.

Silenced Desire and Anger 149

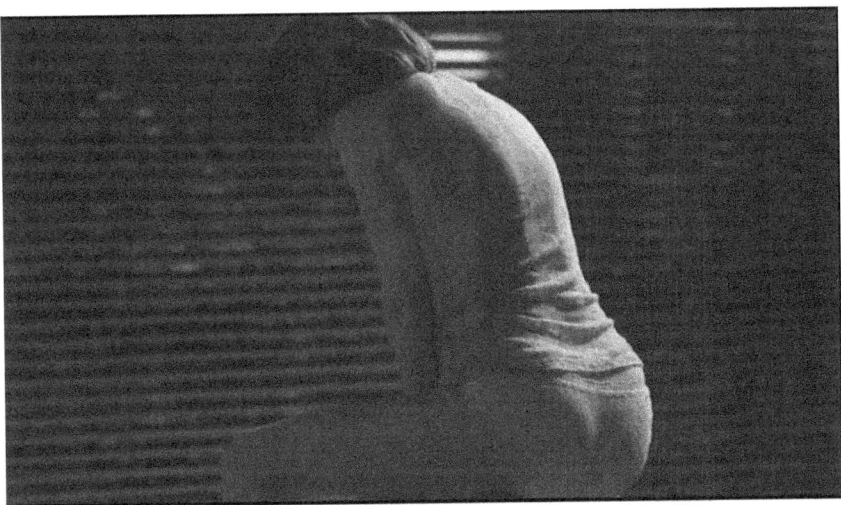

Figure 30 D (Viv Albertine) in beige lace lingerie workshopping a performance in her home studio in *Exhibition*.

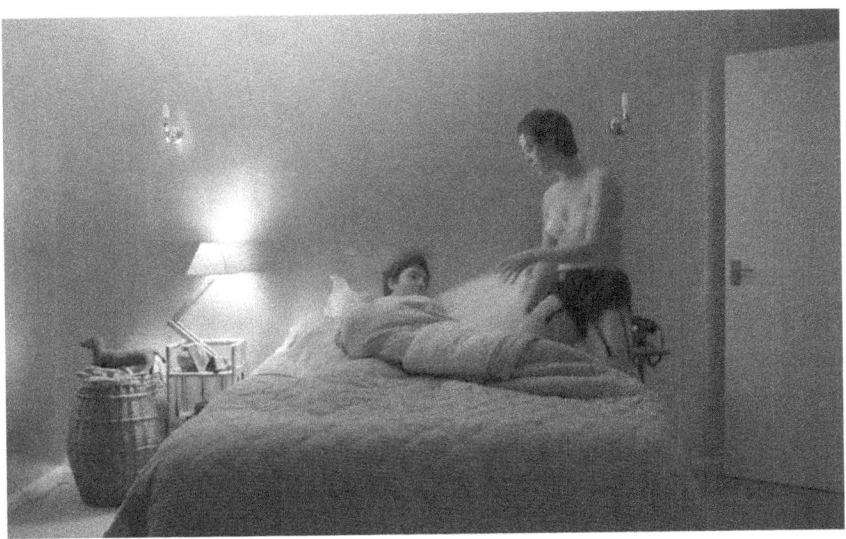

Figure 31 Julie (Honor Swinton Byrne) in the black garter belt in *The Souvenir Part I*.

not—may produce a heightened awareness of one's own sexuality" (2013: 16). The way in which lingerie appears across these three films functions in direct relation to characters' sexual expression. These items of lingerie might be seen to "speak" in a way that suggests an attempt to explore and represent feminine sexuality via a lack of explicit commentary or explanation that might surround the donning of lingerie. Yet, the way in which lingerie is selected and worn in these sequences is not constructed as being for a conventional male viewer in the Mulveyan sense. Even in *The Souvenir Part I*, we learn more about how Julie feels receiving and putting on the garter belt and stockings, than we do Anthony's response to these items. These sequences evoke what it means for characters to select and wear these items as a method for exploring and enhancing their individual sexualities. This sense of a largely silent, self-contained, feminine sexuality also presents itself in *Morvern Callar*, where Morvern shows the boatman the lower half of her body, clad in black stockings and garters. Though Morvern is a younger woman than the characters under discussion in this chapter, she shares something of their sexual and bodily confidence in terms of how she chooses to explore sexual desire and expression.

Silence, Loneliness, and Desire

Ciara Barrett comments that for Hogg, "sound therefore functions to pass comment on the emotionally isolated states-in-space of the narrative subjects of *Unrelated* and *Archipelago*" (Barrett 2015: 12). After Anna has fallen out with the young people, having revealed to Verena that they crashed the borrowed second car, she is side lined at a party at a neighboring villa. Anna drifts on the edges of things, as conversation fills the air. Anna doesn't participate, doesn't speak to anyone, and no one speaks to her. The way that chatter fills up space in this sequence is very much an instance of what Barrett identifies as an example of how sound is used to reinforce Anna's isolation from the family groups.

But, I am also interested in the way that silence functions as a shared space of desire for Anna and Oakley, particularly in their early glances and bodily interactions. At first, when they are introduced, Oakley barely acknowledges Anna. Then later, at dinner, he offers her the cigarette which she declines. As Verena tells the story about Anna and smoking, Oakley observes her carefully. In Figure 32, Oakley looks intrigued by Anna, by her silence, and her closed eyes, that she does not need to offer an explanation, nor does she need to meet his gaze. What this moment ultimately establishes is a sense of

Figure 32 Oakley observes Anna at dinner in *Unrelated*.

affinity between these two characters. This is nowhere more evident than in the profound and flirtatious conversation that takes place in the square in Siena where Anna and Oakley touch on sexual fidelity, the challenge of long-term relationships, the mysteries of attraction, and the decision of whether or not to become a parent. As Barrett and others have observed, Hogg's films are marked by a deliberate technique with regard to silence: "… eschewing background music while augmenting the 'natural' aural topography" (Barrett 2015: 3). So much of Anna and Oakley's interactions have been comprised of glances and physical gestures up to this point. Hogg even reinforces this when the Siena setting is first introduced, filming the two at a distance in the square, as they touch each other, walking to and fro, but not making us party to whatever they are discussing. Verena separates the group, taking Anna off with herself and Badge, while Jack, Oakley, and Archie head off in a different direction. When the group reunites some time later, Anna and Oakley immediately pair off again, at a little distance from the others, and have their most extended conversation. In some ways, this exchange may be viewed as the heart of the film, touching on so many emotive and somewhat taboo topics. The tone of the conversation flows from a flirtatious discussion of the importance of sexual attraction to the question of having children. Oakley asks Anna if Alex is "one of those people who's just not interested" and she looks away, saying "no, no" clearly uncomfortable. Oakley apologizes, realizing he has touched a sensitive topic. He never learns just how sensitive a topic this is for Anna, who later reveals to Verena that she had believed herself pregnant, only to find that she is in fact menopausal.

Silence in *Unrelated* is a field and a repository for desires that cannot be fully articulated or realized, and yet there are so many fascinating gestures that take place between Anna and Oakley; it is almost as if they are not silent at all. Their shared space is not exactly the "aural topography," Barrett identifies, but there is a gestural code that seems to be in operation. Their glances, embraces, narrowing of space all work to create a feeling of intimacy, and their refusal to give things a name adds to the frisson of their attraction.

Archipelago is also filled with silences and gestures, as David Forrest notes:

> A two minute long take frames four characters in medium shot (from left to right: Cynthia, Mother, Christopher and Edward) sitting in the living room, drinking Bloody Marys. Small talk is exchanged about the drinks and the pheasant that they are about to eat, crucially, the scene is *punctuated by two moments of silence*—one which lasts for 20 seconds and precedes a conversation about the celery in the drinks, and another which lasts for 25 seconds, before Rose calls the group to the table. The conspicuous silence and the static nature of the framing draws the viewer towards a more contemplative experience of the narrative as it functions and exists within the frame, as attention moves towards gesture and interaction, or the lack thereof.
>
> (Forrest 2014: 73; my emphasis)

This use of silence as punctuation, as a space for contemplation, allows us to consider the different interpersonal dynamics of the group of people we encounter in *Unrelated* and *Archipelago*. In *Unrelated*, silence is charged with possibility, with the glimmer and snap of eroticism. In contrast, the silence in *Archipelago* is predominantly awkward—it is about family, about class, about the nature of transactional relationships versus the ones that are not. As Barrett has noted, Hogg returns to a set of key themes in her films that concern middle-aged women:

> By focusing on middle-aged women caught in a negotiation of their inclination towards (or feelings of responsibility to desire) motherhood, Hogg's films—*Unrelated*, *Archipelago*, and *Exhibition*—have each interrogated with varying degrees of explicitness narrative themes of maternity and sexuality, which are presented as interdependent, if conflictive, facets of femininity and the "female experience."
>
> (Barrett 2015: 7)

Silence is one of the techniques that Hogg deploys to explore these themes. *Archipelago* is characterized by the awkward silence that exists between family members with different goals. Patricia along with her two adult children Cynthia (Lydia Leonard) and Edward (Tom Hiddleston) have rented a holiday cottage on the Scilly Isles. This is a family holiday organized in part as a send-off for Edward, who is heading to Africa to volunteer for a year. Alongside the family group, there is the hired cook Rose (Amy Lloyd), and Christopher (Christopher W. Baker) a painter and Patricia's watercolor tutor. Rose is introduced via a medium close-up of her aproned mid-section, with her hand holding a cigarette, smoking in the garden. Her quiet, solo cigarette is contrasted with the fractious sibling dynamic of Cynthia and Edward. Cynthia is giving Edward a tough time about his trip to Africa, saying he's "out of step with his generation" and that he should "work like the rest of us"—indicating that she resents both his mobility and his altruism. She describes his decision as "a luxury," and this establishes their different views on the matter. That evening, we see Edward silently undressing and getting into bed. Edward seems faintly uncomfortable in the attic room as he fusses with the collar of his pajamas, and how best to tie the drawstring of his trousers. The narrow room and single bed feel constricting, as if he is slightly too tall for the space, and he is squeezed in but has not even quite realized it himself. His fussing with the pajamas may also indicate he is wearing them as a concession to the family holiday, when he might prefer to wear nothing. It's clear he believes he has taken this room to be agreeable, when in fact he's just making himself uncomfortable. Even though Cynthia has offered him a choice of the larger bedroom she is occupying, it's not quite clear if this is a legitimate choice, and Edward may have opted to take the smaller room in order to give Cynthia one less thing to complain about.

In his bedroom, we also see him writing in a journal. We never see any of this writing, though he later tells Christopher that he writes a lot and thinks he might want to be a writer. This showcasing of what is clearly a private moment recalls the way in which we are also privy to what D does in her bedroom in *Exhibition*. Edward's journal writing is clearly a hidden, personal activity in terms of both the fact that it clearly takes place when he is alone, and the fact that we never see any of his writing.

This motif of unseen work and unheard voices can be traced as a motif across Hogg's work. In *Exhibition*, we never see D's drawings though she is shown drawing on several occasions. These unseen works might also be considered as another technique of silence where characters are shown engaged and even engrossed in activities that remain somewhat private in the sense that they are not fully displayed to the viewer. This is also a technique we see in Hogg in relation to certain kinds of relationships, where we only hear one half of the conversation—a motif that is present in both *Archipelago* and *Unrelated*, where male partners are unseen and unheard. This silencing of the man's perspective in both Patricia's and Anna's long-term heterosexual relationships is clearly a deliberate strategy. Not only do we not hear their voices, these men are completely physically absent from the frame. In this sense, we might see Patricia and Anna as haunted by the spectral presence of their distant partners, whose phone calls often result in frustration and anger. Their phone calls are interruptions to the holiday atmosphere, a reminder of what awaits them when they return to their everyday lives, and the one-sided conversations offer up little sense of compromise or reconciliation. At the end of *Unrelated*, Anna seems to have reconciled with Alex as we see her speaking warmly to him in a taxi on her way to fly home. But *Archipelago*'s conclusion is darker; Patricia finds her patience of many decades finally wearing thin, and her last conversation with William results in her declaring her complete hatred for him.

It is also telling that in both *Unrelated* and *Archipelago*, the women with absent partners temporarily supplant them with other men, though these relationships never quite take on the mantle of an affair. When we see Christopher talking to Patricia and Cynthia about abstraction, it becomes apparent that Patricia has made a particular kind of transactional arrangement—that Christopher's presence is not just about painting and personal tuition, but about the one-on-one attention afforded by his presence. As a woman of a certain age, generation, and class, Cynthia may not feel as if she can access certain forms of attention, but one thing she can do is pay someone to tutor her in painting. In this way, Christopher stands in for William, the absent spouse and father, acting as a kind of paid companion. Rose too functions in this way, a person who has been hired to provide a service. Where Christopher is treated more like a guest, Rose's presence in the house is difficult to negotiate, with her proximity to the family group who have different views about how to treat people who are employees but whose work involves the offering of comfort, food, and hospitality. When Edward suggests they to ask Rose to eat with them, Cynthia dismisses this saying Rose would surely prefer to eat on her own and that Edward doesn't need "to make friends with the cook." Patricia says of Edward "he's just got too much empathy" but both she and Cynthia then feel badly for Rose, as Edward's offers to help with the dishes are clearly not required, and make Rose feel awkward. Cynthia even briefly says she thinks Edward has a bit of a crush on Rose—though again, this is never really made clear. Certainly, Edward spends a good deal of time chatting to Rose, and she does not seem particularly eager to get away from these encounters, but as soon as Cynthia or someone else appears, Rose tends to retreat promptly to the kitchen.

A tension is quickly established vis-à-vis family attitudes to Rose: Cynthia is keen to leave her to her work, while Edward attempts to engage her in conversation, and eventually this extends to him watching her in the kitchen and offering to help with the washing up. Edward is uneasy about what he sees as an unequal relationship, whereas Cynthia and Patricia see Rose very much as someone they've hired, and who is free to go about her own business once her duties have been fulfilled. However, this same attitude doesn't extend to Christopher who doesn't stay with them in the house but does come to meals on occasion. He too is someone who is being paid for his expertise, and yet he is treated far less like an employee.

The tone of the relationship between Christopher and Patricia is established when he asks her whether her husband likes her painting, whether he appreciates this, and she says "if I like it it's a nice thing" but describes Will, her unseen and unheard husband, as "not too strong on imagination." This statement implies that after many years of marriage, Patricia sees her husband clearly, and that she has realized she will not get everything from one person. This is a silence about their marriage, a silence in the form of absence. With her children grown and her husband absent, Patricia has taken up art as the thing that can fill the void. As her one-sided phone conversations with William become increasingly fraught, she moves from a pleasant, conciliatory stance ("it would be very nice if you were with us") and later, increasingly impatient, and finally enraged ("you're so fucking selfish!").

When Edward asks how things are going with the paintings, Patricia responds, "Christopher's pleased, I think that's the main thing." It is a strange response, completely disavowing her own investment in an activity she clearly takes seriously and enjoys enough to engage a private tutor. It reinforces how much Patricia has attached herself to the idea of pleasing a man as a sign of success. Since nothing she does can entice William to join them, there is a sense that she has taken refuge in the idea of pleasing Christopher with her painting accomplishments. There is also a sense of Patricia being unable to recognize her own needs and desires directly, until she finally becomes openly angry with William, where her words finally break open the silence of their marriage. This is in stark contrast to the easy companionship she experiences with Christopher. As can be seen in Figure 33, Patricia sits on the sofa and asks him about whether the artist in him needs more space, a space that might have otherwise been occupied by a family. Christopher answers this rather deep and probing question with warmth and openness: "I kind of regret it but there's lots of children in my life … keeps me silly"; this response does not give too much away, but alludes to a rich kinship network that allows Christopher to experience the fun of having children in his life without being a parent himself. In Figure 33, the smiling laughter of both characters conveys a sense of friendly affinity and trust. The light-heartedness with which this question is received is markedly different than how Anna responds to a similar question in *Unrelated*. For women, this question is culturally loaded, but men can shrug it off, or at the very least, they can respond without stigma. The contrast between Anna's uncomfortable silence versus Christopher's easy response is yet another instance of the way silence can function differently along the axis of gender.

Silenced Desire and Anger

Figure 33 Patricia (Kate Fahy) and Christopher (Christopher W. Baker) in conversation in *Archipelago*.

Some ways through *Archipelago*, we learn that Edward has a girlfriend, Chloe. As he is explaining some of his volunteer training and its restrictions, Cynthia chooses this moment to mention Chloe, Edward's girlfriend of a year and half. Cynthia coldly states "she must be quite worried about you going" but rather than an expression of concern, this seems to be yet another attempt to needle and undermine Edward, to construct his decision as harmfully selfish. Edward reveals Chloe isn't allowed to visit him, as it is a condition of his service that volunteers "lead by example" and aren't seen to engage in premarital sex. He will see Chloe for one night before he leaves for his eleven-month trip. Cynthia asks if they are going to split up, and Edward says he doesn't know why Chloe couldn't be with them now, and Cynthia calmly says "she couldn't really because it's a family holiday" even though Christopher is present at dinner. Cynthia continues to eat, declaring Edward's relationship as clearly important, implying once more that his decision to work abroad is both selfish and frivolous, and yet it is Cynthia who is revealed as invested in a strict maintenance of what and who is family by actively excluding Chloe. Cynthia bites down on some shot, and is suddenly overcome, declaring "it really, really hurts" and storms out. Patricia apologizes to Christopher on everyone's behalf and sends Edward after his sister. He searches the darkening garden, but she has gone off and doesn't return until sometime later, when she explodes in anger at Patricia's attempt to comfort her. Although this confrontation takes place off screen, everyone can hear Cynthia's anger—we see Rose in her room covering her ears. The following morning, Patricia gets her third call from William, and the strain begins to show as she repeatedly declares "I can't bear it" before hanging up on him. At this stage, all the relationships are strained, and yet no one apart from Cynthia is truly expressing their anger.

Edward and Patricia are regularly intimidated into silence by Cynthia and nowhere is this more evident than when they stop for lunch in a deserted restaurant. Cynthia chooses the table and orchestrates where everyone should sit, trying to get Patricia to make a choice or express a preference. As soon as they start to eat, Cynthia declares of her guinea fowl "this isn't done properly" and asks Patricia if hers is alright. Cynthia quickly becomes enraged, in a quiet and terrifying way, calling over the waitress, and asking to speak to the chef. Cynthia is also angry that Patricia is insisting her dish is fine: "You don't have to say it's fine, I'm sending mine back." Everyone else is mortified, and Cynthia, sensing this, declares, "It would be nice if everyone wasn't just sitting in silence." Cynthia is the one dictating the tone of this encounter, and yet the result is everyone else at the table keeping quiet because they don't know how to respond to Cynthia's anger. Rose makes a conciliatory comment, "well, I think you've done the right thing. I think if you're not happy you have the right, as the customer …, " and Cynthia snaps, "Mum and Edward are allergic to any kind of complaining." We can see she is clearly right about this, as witnessed by Edward's discomfort in his too small bedroom and his attempts to weather Cynthia's constant criticism of his choices without getting into a serious argument. Patricia tries to pretend she isn't frustrated and angry with William, and Cynthia is intent on judging everyone, convinced she is always right. The chef appears and explains that guinea fowl is served slightly underdone, but Cynthia maintains her stance: "I wasn't told that when I ordered it." Patricia comments quietly "it's actually rather good" and Edward leaves the table in a huff, his food untouched. The silences of the unresolved family tensions are never really unpacked here.

Edward is clearly angry, but will not verbalize this, preferring instead to storm off (and Cynthia does the same at the penultimate family meal). The only person who does manage to verbalize their anger completely is Patricia, who has a screaming fight over the phone with William, which is overheard by everyone. Back at the holiday cottage, Cynthia and Edward eat dinner while we can hear Patricia yelling over the phone at Will: "you're so fucking selfish!" and finally, "I hate you!" telling him if he doesn't phone Edward tomorrow to say goodbye that neither she nor Edward will ever forgive him. When she returns to the table, neither Cynthia nor Edward remarks on what they have all overheard. Cynthia just says "lasagne's delicious" and then asks "alright?" as Patricia exhales and tries to regain her composure. They all depart the cottage the following day, with no further discussion of this disagreement.

If *Unrelated* is about silence and desire, then *Archipelago* is about silence and anger. Both these films are structured by complex family and kinship dynamics, delineating who belongs in which circles, and the hierarchies that attend each of these holiday arrangements. These are also very much films about class, though this is a subject that is never openly discussed. In *Unrelated*, Verena remarks in passing that the reason she likes to be all together on holiday is that the children are at school and they barely see them, suggesting they are either at a boarding school or away at university, living their own lives. In *Archipelago*, there is a similar sense of gathering the family together, in order to cement a feeling of closeness before Edward goes away for an extended period.

In both *Archipelago* and *Unrelated*, we witness gulfs of silence between close friends and family members. These are characters who are not really used to verbalizing their emotions. It is telling that we only hear one side of things when it comes to the tensions of long-term relationships, and what we hear are the frustrations of women, Anna's and Patricia's. Anger, when it appears, is sharp and terrifying, because Anna and Patricia have finally decided to speak about things that have been bothering them for a long time. For Patricia, this is never really resolved, but for Anna she seems to return to Alex, content that she has purged some of her sadness about where she has found herself. In *Exhibition*, D and H also seem content in the end, having had to work out and through their artistic and personal differences. While there is a sense of anger and frustration having broken through the silence in these films, desire remains unresolved. Anna and Oakley have already given each other their attention and proof of desire, and perhaps that is all they require from one another. The exchange of looks and touches is what is important in *Unrelated*, the being seen, not what they say to each other that remains the most compelling aspect of silence in this film.

Afterword

To know how to use your words is one thing, but do you know how to use your gaze? That is the question these films are asking and trying to answer. Looking back and looking at each other is a way of looking for more, because just being looked at is not even close to enough and the silences in these films create the space for something more to happen. In *Paul Takes the Form of a Mortal Girl*, we learn "Just look back; that was the whole trick" (Andrea Lawlor 2017: 31). The trick is flirtation, and achieving reciprocated desire, not just attention. For Paul, the protagonist that can shapeshift their gender presentation at will, gazing back constitutes a radical act of visibility. To look, turn away, then look back to meet a gaze turn flirtation into a method for reshaping what it means to look and be looked at. No longer simply a one-way channel, the cinematic gaze can become something other than what we have imagined is possible. In the hands of these directors, these powerful silences act to enable a gaze that can shapeshift to allow a more generous reciprocity.

While writing this book, I have thought a great deal about what it means to use your gaze to make a space for someone. Some of this thinking has happened because I have been given this kind of space, and because I have made it for others. Silence, like desire or beauty, is a gift. It is a gift of a space for noticing, looking, gazing, and listening. It's a space for knowing you don't have to say anything, or for wrestling with feelings that are hard to articulate. In these films, silence becomes the space and the texture that allows the unspoken and taboo to be explored and portrayed. Their silences are far from the ineffable, the falling silent of the artist who has nothing more to say. Instead, the silences here are contemplative, but also confrontational in what they show. They can contain horror but also voluptuousness, and this capaciousness stretches from the tension held by the girls of *Innocence* as they know they are watched, right through to the enveloping, reciprocal gazes of *Portrait of a Lady on Fire*. The silence and quiet in the work of these directors ask us to listen, and detain our gaze. In her blistering, brilliant book *Art Monsters: Unruly Bodies in Feminist*

Art, Lauren Elkin states, "If there is a female gaze, it is not an attribute of any art made by women, but something that attempts to express what it means to live in a female body—whatever form it might take" (2023: 53). In the work of these directors, there is the look, the stare, and then there is the gaze which can work any way we want it to. Those shared gazes are what is most important and what is most radical—that's what the silence is there to foster, it's there to get us to notice our own bodies and to notice how we can look at each other, reminding us as Julia Bell argues, "Our bodies need to know that they are noticed by other human bodies, if for nothing else than to be reassured that we exist" (Bell 2020: 18). This shared looking and listening is a plea for both nuance and care. This new cinema of silence and shared gazing can be practiced by anyone, and I look forward to seeing who else is out there.

References

Ahmed, Sara. *Living a Feminist Life*. London and New York: Duke University Press, 2017.

Alexander, Jonathan. "Being Cruised." *Los Angeles Review of Books*, October 2, 2018. https://lareviewofbooks.org/article/being-cruised/

Artt, Sarah. "Being inside Her Silence: Silence and Performance in Lynne Ramsay's *Morvern Callar*." *Scope: An Online Journal of Film and Television Studies* (February 2013): 1–13.

Artt, Sarah. "Sex Sounds: On Aural Explicitness in *Call Me by Your Name*: Perspectives on the Film." Ed. Edward Lamberti and Michael Williams. Bristol: Intellect, 2024.

Bacholle, Michèle. "For a Fluid Approach to Céline Sciamma's *Portrait of a Lady on Fire*." *French Cultural Studies* (2022): 1–14. DOI: 10.1177/09571558221099637

Barnes, Djuna. *Nightwood*. London: Faber and Faber, [1936] 2007.

Barratt, Ciara. "The Feminist Cinema of Joanna Hogg: Melodrama, Female Space, and the Subversion of Phallogocentric Metanarrative." *Alphaville Journal of Film and Screen Media* (2015): 129–44. DOI: 10.33178/alpha.10.08

Barukh, Sarah. "Hello, Selfie! Kate Durbin on Selfie Culture and the Girl Gaze." *Fem Magazine*, February 24, 2016. https://femmagazine.com/hello-selfie-kate-durbin-on-selfie-culture-and-the-girl-gaze/

Batuman, Elif. "Céline Sciamma's Quest for a New, Feminist Grammar of Cinema." *The New Yorker*, January 31, 2022. https://www.newyorker.com/magazine/2022/02/07/celine-sciammas-quest-for-a-new-feminist-grammar-of-cinema

Bell, Julia. *Radical Attention*. London: Peninsula Press, 2020.

Bigunet, John. *Silence*. New York and London: Bloomsbury, 2015.

Bradbury-Rance, Clara. *Lesbian Cinema after Queer Theory*. Edinburgh: Edinburgh University Press, 2019.

Brennan, Summer. *High Heel*. New York and London: Bloomsbury, 2019.

Carter, Angela. "The Company of Wolves." In *Burning Your Boats: The Collected Short Stories of Angela Carter*. London: Penguin, 1997, 212–20.

Citron, Michelle, et al. "Women and Film: A Discussion of Feminist Aesthetics." *New German Critique* 13 (1978): 83–107.

Cixous, Hélène, Keith Cohen, and Paula Cohen. "Laugh of the Medusa." *Signs* 1, no. 4 (Summer, 1976): 875–93.

Colette. *Chéri* [1920] and *The Last of Chéri* [1926]. Trans. Roger Senhouse. Middlesex: Penguin, 1954.

Creed, Barbara. *The Monstrous Feminine: Feminism, Film, Psychoanalysis*. London and New York: Routledge, 1993.

de Luca, Tiago and Nuno Barradas Jorge (eds.). *Slow Cinema*. Edinburgh: Edinburgh University Press, 2016.

Despentes, Virginie. *King Kong Theory*. Trans. Sophie Benson. New York: The Feminist Press, [2006] 2010.

Dittmar, Linda. "The Articulating Self: Difference as Resistance in *Black Girl, Ramparts of Clay*, and *Salt of the Earth*." In *Multiple Voices in Feminist Film Criticism*. Ed. Diane Carson, Linda Dittmar, and Janice R. Welsch. Minneapolis and London: University of Minneapolis Press, 1994, 391–405.

Driscoll, Catherine. *Girls: Feminine Adolescence in Popular Culture and Cultural Theory*. New York: Columbia University Press, 2002.

Elkin, Lauren. *Flâneuse: Women Walk the City in Paris, New York, Tokyo, Venice and London*. London: Chatto and Windus, 2016.

Elkin, Lauren. *Art Monsters: Unruly Bodies in Feminist Art*. London: Chatto and Windus, 2023.

Ernaux, Annie. *Passion Simple*. Paris: Éditions Gallimard, 1991.

Ernaux, Annie. *Getting Lost/Se Perdre*. Trans. Alison L. Strayer. London: Fitzcarraldo, 2022.

Fife Donaldson, Lucy. "Feeling and Filmmaking: The Design and Affect of Film Sound." *The New Soundtrack* 7, no. 1 (2017): 31–46.

Figgis, Mike. "Silence: The Absence of Sound." In *Soundscape: The School of Sound Lectures, 1998-2001*. Ed. Larry Sider, Diane Freeman, and Jerry Sider. London and New York: Wallflower Press, 2003, 9–13.

Forrest, David. "The Films of Joanna Hogg: New British Realism and Class." *Studies in European Cinema* 11, no. 1 (2014): 64–75. DOI: 10.1080/17411548.2014.903102

Galt, Rosalind. *Pretty: Film and the Decorative Image*. New York: Columbia University Press, 2011.

Gill, Rosalind. "Empowerment/Sexism: Figuring Female Sexual Agency in Contemporary Advertising." *Feminism and Psychology* 18, no. 1 (2008): 35–60. Doi: 10.1177/0959353507084950

Halberstam, Jack. *Skin Shows: Gothic Horror and the Technology of Monsters*. Durham and London: Duke University Press, 1995.

Hallam, Julia. "Inappropriate Desires? Sex and the (Ageing) Single Girl." *Journal of British Cinema and Television* 13, no. 4 (2016): 552–70.
Hartman, Saidiya. *Wayward Lives, Beautiful Experiments*. London: Serpent's Tail, 2019.
Heti, Sheila. *Motherhood*. London: Harvill Secker, 2018.
Hinchliff, Sharon. "Sexing up the Midlife Woman: Cultural Representations of Ageing, Femininity and the Sexy Body." In *Ageing, Popular Culture and Contemporary Feminism: Harleys and Hormones*. Ed. Imelda Whelehan and Joel Gwynne. London: Palgrave Macmillan, 2014, 63–77.
Horton, Justin. "The Unheard Voice in Sound Film." *Cinema Journal* 52, no. 4 (2013): 3–24.
Johnson, Lisa. "Perverse Angle: Feminist Film, Queer Film, Shame." *Signs: Journal of Women in Culture and Society* 30, no. 1 (2004): 1361–84.
Kaplan, E. Ann. "Women, Trauma, and Late Modernity: Sontag, Duras, and Silence in Cinema, 1960–1980." *Framework: The Journal of Cinema and Media* 50, no. 1/2 (2009): 158–75. http://www.jstor.org/stable/41552545
Koepnick, Lutz. *On Slowness: Towards an Aesthetic of the Contemporary*. New York: Columbia University Press, 2014.
Kristeva, Julia. *Powers of Horror: An Essay on Abjection*. Trans. Leon S. Roudiez. New York: Columbia University Press, 1982.
Lachman, Kathryn M. "Wonder and Loss in Céline Sciamma's *Petite Maman*." *French Cultural Studies*, no. 0 (2023): 1–14.
Lawlor, Andrea. *Paul Takes the Form of a Mortal Girl*. London: Picador, 2017.
Lebeau, Vicky. *Childhood and Cinema*. London: Reaktion Books, 2008.
Leduc, Violette. *Thérèse and Isabelle*. Trans. Sophie Lewis. London: Salammbo Press, 2012.
Lindner, Katharina. "Spectacular Dis-embodiments: The Female Dancer on Film." *Scope: An Online Journal of Film and Television Studies*, no. 20, June 2011. https://www.nottingham.ac.uk/scope/documents/2011/june-2011/lindner.pdf
Lindner, Katharina. *Film Bodies: Queer Feminist Encounters with Gender and Sexuality in Cinema*. London: I.B. Tauris, 2018.
Lorde, Audre. *Your Silence Will Not Protect You*. London: Silver Press, 2017.
Maitland, Sara. *A Book of Silence*. London: Granta Books, 2008.
Mayer, So. *Holy Tilda Swinton* 2015. http://cleojournal.com/2015/11/24/holy-tilda-swinton/
Mayer, So. *Political Animals: The New Feminist Cinema*. London: I.B. Tauris, 2016.
McCann, Hannah. *Queering Femininity: Sexuality, Feminism, and the Politics of Presentation*. London and New York: Routledge, 2018.

Michelsen Foy, George. *Zero Decibels: The Quest for Absolute Silence*. New York and London: Scribner: 2010.

Mroz, Matilda. "Performing Evolution: Immersion, Unfolding and Lucile Hadžhalilović's *Innocence*." In *Slow Cinema*. Ed. Tiago de Luca and Nun Barradas Jorge. Edinburgh: Edinburgh University Press, 2016, 287–98.

Nelson, Maggie. *The Art of Cruelty: A Reckoning*. New York and London: W.W. Norton, 2011.

Nelson, Maggie. *The Argonauts*. London: Melville House, 2015.

Parsons, Deborah L. *Streetwalking the Metropolis: Women, the City and Modernity*. Oxford: Oxford University Press, 2000.

Pisters, Patricia. *New Blood in Contemporary Cinema: Women Directors and the Poetics of Horror*. Edinburgh: Edinburgh University Press, 2020.

Prochnik, George. *In Pursuit of Silence: Listening for Meaning in a World of Noise*. London and New York: Anchor Books, 2011.

Quinlivan, Davina. "An Architecture of Light and Air, a Rhythm of Stillness: Absence in Joanna Hogg's Exhibition." *Screening the Past*, no. 43, April 2018. http://www.screeningthepast.com/issue-43-dossier-materialising-absence-in-film-and-media/an-architecture-of-light-and-air-a-rhythm-of-stillness-absence-in-joanna-hoggs-exhibition/

Rhys, Jean. *Voyage in the Dark*. Harmondsworth, Middlesex: Penguin, 1934.

Rhys, Jean. *Quartet*. London: Penguin Books, [1928] 1973.

Rhys, Jean. *The Collected Short Stories*. New York and London: Norton, 1987.

Rowe Karlyn, Kathleen. *Unruly Girls Unrepentant Mothers*. Austin, Texas: University of Texas Press, 2011.

Russell, Legacy. *Glitch Feminism: A Manifesto*. New York and London: Verso, 2020.

Russo, Mary. *The Female Grotesque*. New York and London: Routledge, 1994.

Scalway, Helen. "The Contemporary Flâneuse." In *The Invisible Flâneuse? Gender, Public, Space and Visual Culture in Nineteenth-Century Paris*. Ed. Aruna D'Souza and Tom McDonough. Manchester: Manchester University Press, 2006, 168–71.

Shepherd, Simon. "Erotic Silence." *Performance Research* 4, no. 3 (1999): 34–9. DOI: 10.1080/13528165.1999.10871690

Sim, Stuart. *Manifesto for Silence: Confronting the Politics and Culture of Noise*. Edinburgh: Edinburgh University Press, 2007.

Smyth, Sarah Louise. "Postfeminism, Ambivalence and the Mother in Lynne Ramsay's *We Need to Talk About Kevin* (2011)." *Film Criticism* 44, no. 1 (2020): 1–17. DOI: 10.3998/fc.13761232.0044.106

Sontag, Susan. *Against Interpretation and Other Essays*. London: Penguin, [1961] 2009.

Sontag, Susan. *Styles of Radical Will*. London: Penguin, [1966] 2009.

Srinivasan, Amia. *The Right to Sex*. London: Bloomsbury, 2022.

Théberge, Paul. "Almost Silent: The Interplay of Sound and Silence in Contemporary Cinema and Television." In *Lowering the Boom: Critical Studies in Film Sound*. Ed. Jay Beck and Tony Grajeda. Urbana and Chicago: University of Illinois Press, 2008, 51–67.

Thornham, Sue. *What If I Had Been the Hero? Investigating Women's Cinema*. London: BFI/Palgrave Macmillan, 2012.

Thornham, Sue. "A Hatred so Intense ….We Need to Talk About Kevin, Postfeminism, and Women's Cinema." *Sequence: Serial Studies in Media, Film, and Music* 2, no. 1 (2013). https://reframe.sussex.ac.uk/sequence2/archive/sequence-2-1/

Träger, Eike. "Symbolic Matricide Gone Awry: On Absent and—Maybe Even Worse—Present Mothers in Horror Movies." In *The Absent Mother in the Cultural Imagination*. Ed. B. Åström. Cham: Palgrave Macmillan, 2017, 207–22. DOI: 10.1007/978-3-319-49037-3_13

Tsaousi, Christiana and Joanna Brewis. "Are You Feeling Special Today? Underwear and the 'Fashioning' of Female Identity." *Culture and Organization* 19, no. 1 (2013): 1–21. DOI: 10.1080/14759551.2011.634196

Vogelin, Salomé. *Listening to Noise and Silence: Towards a Philosophy of Sound Art*. London and New York: Continuum, 2010.

Walsh, Joanna. *Break.up*. London: Tuskar Rock Press, 2018.

Walsh, Joanna. *Girl Online: A User Manifesto*. London: Verso, 2022.

Warhol, Robyn R. and Diane Price Herndl. *Feminisms: An Anthology of Literary Theory and Criticism. Revised Edition*. New Brunswick, New Jersey: Rutgers University Press, 1997.

Warner, Marina. "Afterword." In *The Debutante and Other Stories*. Ed. Leonora Carrington. London: Silver Press, 2017, 146–53.

Williams, Linda. "Film Bodies: Gender, Genre, Excess." In *Feminist Film Theory: A Reader*. Ed. Sue Thornham. Edinburgh: Edinburgh University Press, 1991/1999, 267–81.

Williams, Linda. "A Jury of Their Peers: Questions of Silence, Speech, and Judgement in Marleen Gorris's *A Question of Silence*." In *Multiple Voices in Feminist Film Criticism*. Ed. Diane Carson, Linda Dittmar, and Janice R. Welsch. Minneapolis and London: University of Minneapolis Press, 1994, 432–40.

Wilson, Elizabeth. *The Sphinx in the City*. London: Virago, 1991.

Wilson, Emma. "Scenes of Hurt and Rapture: Céline Sciamma's *Girlhood*." *Film Quarterly* 70, no. 3 (2017): 10–22.

Wilson, Emma. *The Reclining Nude: Agnès Varda, Catherine Breillat, and Nan Goldin*. Liverpool: Liverpool University Press, 2019.

Wilson, Emma. *Céline Sciamma: Portraits*. Edinburgh: Edinburgh University Press, 2021.

Wolff, Janet. *Feminine Sentences: Essays on Women and Culture*. Cambridge and Oxford: Polity Press, 1990.

Zambreno, Kate. *Heroines*. Semiotexte/Cambridge, MA and London, England: South Pasadena California/MIT Press, 2012.

Zarzycka, Marta. "Showing Sounds: Listening to War Photographs." In *Carnal Aesthetics: Transgressive Imagery and Feminist Politics*. Ed. Bettina Papenburg and Marta Zarzycka. London: I.B. Tauris, 2013, 42–53.

Index

abandoned sound 18
adolescence 41, 51, 65, 67, 70
    puberty 73, 76
    romance 71
    sexuality 73
age 3–5, 43, 69–71, 74, 140–2, 147
Ahmed, Sara 41, 60
Alexander, Jonathan 142
anger 29, 74, 120, 127, 133–4, 137, 141, 158–60
Archipelago (Hogg) 12
    absence of dialogue 139
    absent partners 154–7
    male presence 38
    middle-aged women 152–3
    occupation 139
    silence and anger 22, 152–3, 159
    water features 36
art/artwork 7–8, 15, 77–8, 95, 108, 114
Art Monsters: Unruly Bodies in Feminist Art (Elkin) 161–2

Bacholle, Michèle 35
Barnes, Djuna 1
Barrett, Ciara 113, 137, 150–2
Being Cruised (Alexander) 142
Bell, Julia 162
Bigunet, John 9–10, 13
A Book of Silence (Maitland) 9–10
Bradbury-Rance, Clara 69
Break.up (Walsh) 97
Brennan, Summer 46, 97

Chéri (Colette) 96–8
childhood 41, 49, 60, 68, 73, 80, 87, 103, 131–2
cinema 14. *See also* horror cinema
    abandoned sound 18
    environmental noises 11–13, 15, 21
    lesbian 69

musical/dialogue silences 21–2, 68, 82, 90, 116–18, 139, 141
    semi-public locations 70
    young actors protection 77–8
Cixous, Hélène 112
Colette 96–7
"The Company of Wolves" (Carter) 83
Cotter, Holland 7
Creed, Barbara 115, 126

desire 9–10, 12, 23–7, 67–71, 77, 150–60
    feminine 94, 144–5
    maternal desire 126–7
    queer 71, 76
    sexual desire with 112–14, 143–4
    unexpected desires 79–81
Dittmar, Linda 20, 81
Driscoll, Catherine 70, 72–3, 76, 80, 83, 85
Durbin, Kate 67

Earwig (Hadžhalilović) 11
emergent personhood 41, 62
Evolution (Hadžhalilović) 11
    boys of 53–5, 58
    caregiving figures 54–6, 127–30, 132
    child gaze 55
    food, abjection 131–3
    horror/threat 57, 71
    hospital workers 55–7
    maternal vessel 131–2
    motherhood 115, 127–9, 131–2, 135–6
    nature place 28
    silent rituals 55–8
    stares 22
    swimming activity 57
    water features 36, 41–2, 53–4
Exhibition (Hogg) 22
    absence of dialogue 139
    art/drawings 98, 108, 111

bodily pleasure 108, 112–13
desiring gazes in 96
flaneuse 98
nudity 109–10
sexual identity/desire 31, 109, 110, 112, 148–9
water features 36
women in public 107, 114
work and personal tension 113–14

fear 11, 23, 83, 110
Figgis, Mike 19–20
flâneuse 94–107
Forrest, David 152

gaze 2–3, 5, 23–7, 67–8, 79–81, 143, 161–2
  child gaze 41–2, 49–52, 55, 132
  collaborative 101, 110
  curious 73, 87
  desiring gazes 71, 96
  nurturing 69
  queer girl gaze 76, 83
  shamed/lowered 105, 110, 142
  surveilling/nurturing 69
gender 26–7, 58–61, 76
Gill, Rosalind 94
girlhood 67, 69–70, 73–4
  extra-diegetic soundtrack. 82
Girlhood/Bande des Filles (Sciamma) 28
  absence of dialogue 68, 82, 90
  dance 85
  desire 69–70
  gazes, looks, and stares 67–8
  longing and loss 30
  male presence 38
  music and silence in 82–3
  self-knowledge 87
  space and 83–6
  threat 84
  water features 36

Hadžhalilović, Lucile 3, 10–12, 22, 41–2, 44, 51, 59, 65, 67, 71, 115
Halberstam, Jack 17–18
Hallam, Julia 144
Heti, Sheila 107, 115, 125, 133
Hinchliff, Sharon 137

Hogg, Joanna 3, 11, 22, 31, 34, 36–7, 110, 136–7, 139–40, 137, 139–40, 143–4, 150–4
horror cinema 23, 57, 83, 116, 120–1, 123, 136

identity(ies) 69, 87–8, 102, 108
Innocence (Hadžhalilović) 10–11, 132, 139, 161
  child gaze 41–2, 49–52
  curiosity 46–51, 73
  desires 49
  fairy-tale quality 42–3, 46
  girlhood 43–8, 71, 74
  nature place 28
  protection/reassurance 45
  rules for girl 43–5
  sexuality 49–50
  stares 22
  surveillance 52–3
  swimming rules 43–4
  violence 46
  water features 41–4

Johnson, Lisa 103, 142

Kaplan, E. Ann 14–15, 19
King Kong Theory (Despentes) 26, 129
Koepnick, Lutz 5
Kristeva, Julia 119, 131–2

"The Laugh of the Medusa" (Cixous) 112
Leaving Las Vegas (Figgis) 19
LeBeau, Vicky 51
Leduc, Violette 71, 78–9
lesbianism 67–9
Lindner, Katharina 52, 58–60, 64, 69, 85, 134–5
Listening to Noise and Silence (Voegelin) 15
look 7, 22–4, 27, 29, 34, 42, 48, 54, 56, 64, 68, 70, 75–7, 87–8, 97–8, 111, 138, 141–2
Lorde, Audre 3
Lowe, Alice 126

Maitland, Sara 10–15
A Manifesto for Silence (Sim) 13
Michelsen Foy, George 9, 12–13

Morvern Callar (Ramsay) 4, 6, 15, 105
  absence of dialogue 116–18
  accomplishment/achievement 38
  artist-exhibitionist identity 98, 101–3, 105–7
  desiring gazes in 96
  friendship 103
  lowered gaze 110
  music streaming 103–4
  nudity 110
  quiet soundscape 98
  sexuality 30
  shamed/lowered gaze 105
  sound design 117–18
  threat 99
  water features 36
  women in public 95, 100–1, 114
motherhood 28–9, 115–16, 118–20, 122–32, 136
Mroz, Matilda 42
Mulvey, Laura 2, 4
musical/dialogue silences 21–2
Mysterious Skin (Araki) 69

Nelson, Maggie 54, 123
Nightwood, (Barnes) 1
nurturing gaze 69

Paul Takes the Form of a Mortal Girl (Lawlor) 161
Petite Maman (Sciamma) 27–8
Pisters, Patricia 128
Portrait of a Lady on Fire/Portrait de la jeune fille en feu (Sciamma) 4, 24
  desire and risk 24–6, 34
  fluids features 37
  intimacy 110
  male presence 38
  sexuality 34–5, 78
Powers of Horror (Kristeva) 11, 131
Pretty: Film and the Decorative Image (Galt) 145
Prochnik, George 12–13
punishing gaze 75–6

Quartet (Rhys) 1, 97
  desire 71, 76, 80
  gaze 74, 76, 83

  identities 87–8
  liberation 69
  queer 67–71
A Question of Silence/De stilte rond Christine M (Gorris) 16–17, 19–20

Ramsay, Lynne 3, 21, 99, 102–3, 110, 116, 121
The Reclining Nude (Wilson) 118
Rhys, Jean 1, 96–7, 100–1
Russell, Legacy 27
Russo, Mary 131

Sand, Georges 95
Scalway, Helen 98, 100
Sciamma, Céline 3–4, 7, 11, 22, 26, 28–9, 35, 38, 41, 51, 59, 65, 67, 70, 74, 78, 84–5, 132
sexuality 30–1, 34–5, 49–50, 69–70, 73, 94
  sexual desire 112, 143, 150
  sexual practice 148–50
sex worker 95, 100–1
Shepherd, Simon 78, 93–4, 109–12
silence 1, 15–16
  children's fear 11
  in cinema 14, 20–1, 137
  contemporary art 2
  disruptive power 5
  environment/way of living 11–13, 15
  erotic silence 78
  gazes 3, 5, 161
  gender 26–7
  harmful and complicit 4
  health benefits 14
  illicit affinity 137
  masculinity 93
  musical/dialogue 21–2
  slowness and 5–8
  small talk 137
  solo working 137
  system of oppression 67
  textures of 1–2, 4, 21, 69, 118
  valuing of 20
  women and 2–4, 14–16, 93
"Silence is Golden" (Casal) 22
The Silences of the Palace/Samt al-qusur (Tlatli) 18–20

Sim, Stuart 3, 13
Smyth, Sarah Louise 122
Solnit, Rebecca 3
Sontag, Susan 2, 4, 22, 77
The Souvenir Part I and *II* (Hogg) 4, 31–4
    bliss/euphoria 37
    motherhood 135–6
    physical desires 37
    sexual practice 148–50
stare 7–8, 16, 22–5, 42, 49–50, 54, 65, 68, 70, 80, 82, 123–4, 146, 162
surveilling gaze 42, 52, 69

The Tango Lesson (Potter) 113
Théberge, Paul 20–1, 44
Thérèse and Isabelle (Leduc) 71, 78
Thornham, Sue 124
to-be-looked-at-ness 2, 5
Tomboy (Sciamma) 7, 134
    absence of music 82
    binary gender 58–61
    child gaze 59, 64–5
    motherhood 134–6
    open attitude 64
    self-boying 59–60, 87–8
    swimming outing 61–2
    water features 36
toxic looks 75–7
Träger, Eike 120–1

Under the Skin (Adler) 99–101, 105
Unrelated (Hogg) 10–11, 136
    absence of dialogue 141
    absent partners 154–6
    anger and desire 29–31, 143
    child-free status 138
    flirtation works 142
    gazes 143, 150–1
    intimacy 142–3, 147
    male presence 38
    mature female desire 144–5
    occupation 139
    self-confidence 147
    self-evaluation 138
    sexual practice 148–50
    silence and desire 22, 159
    stares 143, 146

teenagers party 140–1
water features 36
urban noise 12–13

video essay format 21–2
violence 16–18, 46, 54, 70, 118
visual doubling 119–20
Voegelin, Salomé 5, 15
Voyage in the Dark (Rhys) 100–1

Walsh, Joanna 67, 78, 97, 137
Warner, Marina 1
Water Lilies/Naissance des pieuvres (Sciamma)
    adolescence 67, 70
    cultural dissonance 73
    desiring girl gazes 69–71
    English/French title of 70–1
    feminine bodies 79, 81
    friendships 67, 76, 81
    girlhood 67, 69, 73–4
    harassment 74
    longing and loss 30
    looks, stares, shared gazes 68, 70, 80
    nurturing gaze 69
    punishing gaze 75–6
    queer girl gaze 67–8
    self-actualization 49, 68, 78
    surveilling gaze 69
    toxic looks 75–7
    unexpected desires 79
    verbal silence 68–9
    water features 36, 71–2, 79–81
We Need to Talk About Kevin (Ramsay)
    anger and desire 29, 133–4
    bodily abandonment 119
    horror movie 116, 123, 136
    infant care 124–5
    La Tomatina festival 116–17
    malevolence 120
    maternal status 122–3
    motherhood 115–16, 118–20, 122, 125, 127
    sound design 117–18
    stares 123–4
    teenage bond 126

unlikeableness 133–4
violence 118
visual doubling 119–20
water features 36–7
"When Words Fail" (Verdeure) 22
Williams, Linda 16–17, 23
Wilson, Elizabeth 94–5
Wilson, Emma 82–4, 90, 118

womanhood 70–1
woman's silence 1–2, 4, 93
women's sexual power 94–5

Zambreno, Kate 73–4
Zarzycka, Marta 2
Zero Decibels: The Quest for Absolute Silence (Foy) 9

www.ingramcontent.com/pod-product-compliance
Lightning Source LLC
Chambersburg PA
CBHW052047300426
44117CB00012B/2012